Living L'Arche

Living L'Arche

Stories of Compassion, Love, and Disability

KEVIN S. REIMER

LITURGICAL PRESS
Collegeville, Minnesota

www.litpress.org

Published for the United States of America and Canada by
LITURGICAL PRESS
Collegeville, Minnesota 56321

First published 2009

British Library Cataloguing-in-Publication Data
A catalogue record for this book is available from the British Library.

ISBN 978-0-8146-3299-4

Typeset by Kenneth Burnley, Wirral, Cheshire
Printed and bound in Great Britain by The Cromwell Press Group, Wiltshire

Contents

For Larry

Foreword

In our L'Arche communities we live together: people with disabilities and people who for one reason or another come to be with them. We eat together, we work together, we have fun together, we pray together and sometimes fight together. People with disabilities are often called the *core members* of the community; those who come to live with them are often called *assistants*, and they come for a few weeks, or months, or years, or a lifetime.

What is it like to live together? Here is an excellent book that will tell you what it is all about and how it really is. Kevin Reimer does not tell us the theory or the vision behind the life. He listens to the stories of assistants who are in the various L'Arche communities of the United States. They tell us what they are living in a very realistic way.

Kevin shows that they come to L'Arche because they are searching to live a life of meaningful relationships. The core members who have suffered from rejection and feelings of shame are crying out for authentic relationships. They can then become the teachers of love and healers of the searching assistants and sometimes of their broken hearts. They help the assistants grow to greater maturity; they lead the way into a deepened vision of Christianity, a way of unity and of love.

These stories are not idealized – far from it. They tell of the pains and the joys, the frustrations, the conflicts, the angers of the assistants, but also of their transformation and growth. This book tells us how it really is.

And it is amazing! Life in these communities, as it is told, is a revelation of what our society could become if we were prepared to live a relationship with people who are weaker and more vulnerable. The so-called weak and the strong can heal each other through a bonding of compassion and love. They can give life to each other and help each other to become more fully human.

Kevin does not stop at the stories, however interesting and enlightening they are. He leads us into a reflection of what is happening in people, and how the healing and transformation are taking place in them and at

vii

what level. He links the experiences of assistants to a vision given through human sciences. He shows us from a very human point of view the meaning of L'Arche, but also of the human person. All of us are vulnerable, all of us are fragile. So our L'Arche communities are also necessarily vulnerable and fragile. If people seek to listen to the inner voice of God, then L'Arche will continue as a place of healing, growth and hope.

This book is not only important for people in L'Arche, but also for all those who want to know more about it and all those who are searching for a new way to live in our broken and divided world.

Jean Vanier
Trosly-Breuil, France

Prologue

To Mercy, Pity, Peace, and Love
All pray in their distress;
And to these virtues of delight
Return their thankfulness.

For Mercy, Pity, Peace, and Love
Is God, our father dear,
And Mercy, Pity, Peace, and Love
Is Man, his child and care.

For Mercy has a human heart,
Pity a human face,
And Love, the human form divine,
And Peace, the human dress.

Then every man, of every clime,
That prays in his distress,
Prays to the human form divine,
Love, Mercy, Pity, Peace.

And all must love the human form,
In heathen, turk, or jew;
Where Mercy, Love, and Pity dwell
There God is dwelling too.

*(William Blake, 'The Divine Image',
from* Songs of Innocence, *1789)*

1

Downward Mobility

For I have heard the sound thereof; should I not turn with yearning eyes, turn earthwards with a pitiful pang?

(Christina Rossetti)[1]

Incense drifts in ribbons from the altar. A tall priest in ivory vestments stands before the communion table. The downtown cathedral is packed with dignitaries, neighbors, and friends. On my lap rests a funeral program in lavender parchment. The list of speakers is impressive. A city supervisor is followed by a ranking corporate executive who precedes the local bishop. Their remarks are a moving retrospective of the deceased – praise for a man of uncommon insight, wisdom, and compassionate love. His accomplishments are many, his example inspiring. While among the living, Robert exhorted others to care deeply and passionately for the underprivileged. He was a fixture in the local Catholic parish. Young and old knew his warbling tenor and sanguine preference for older hymns. The service ends with a slideshow of Robert's life. Photographs map the usual territory of home, work, and vacation. Joy and happiness are transparent through the images. The gravity of remembrance suggests the deceased might have been a mayor of this great city, or perhaps a renowned author. Such is not the case. The prominent face in the slideshow is that of a middle-aged gentleman with Down's syndrome.[2]

Robert is gone. Yet his relational fingerprints abide. Along with some 15 others, he was a disabled 'core member' living in community with caregiver 'assistants'. His community is known as L'Arche (French for 'the Ark'). Fittingly, these homes preserve human dignity in a turbulent and impersonal world. L'Arche is an international movement of residential communities for the developmentally disabled and their caregivers. More than a service organization, L'Arche is about the discovery and practice of compassionate love. The surprise inversion of Robert's life example is no accident. His passing confers a great secret. Authentic compassion is only

3

distantly related to individual talent or will. The gift of care supersedes fair exchange and individual benefit. Unexpectedly, compassionate love is learned from disabled persons living at the furthest margins of modern society.

The priest gives a benediction ending the funeral mass. Congregants move into aisles and through massive oaken doors at the rear of the cathedral. The crowd makes progress slow. An assistant from Robert's community shuffles next to me. Her name is Marilyn. We talk informally about L'Arche. Her comments offer clues regarding the origins of compassionate love and the people who animate its practice.

You know, I am a thoughtful person. I read a lot. My first introduction to L'Arche was through the writings of Jean Vanier [founder of L'Arche]. He's written dozens of books. One of the things he talks about is something called *downward mobility*; the idea that our deepest human potential lives in simple relationships. These relationships include the disabled and the poor. According to Vanier, our world has things backward. We are told that upward mobility should be our fulfillment. Things like financial success, large homes, fancy cars, status in our work. But this only blinds us to what really matters. Most of us live in L'Arche because we're attracted to the idea of downward mobility.

I have an affinity for people who are marginalized. I am very sensitive to people's feelings, probably more than their thoughts. I believe personality is more of what people emote than what they are thinking. I'm very interested in the spiritual journey and what is going on beneath the surface. Just like all those Californians. [laughs.] I am most concerned with the welfare of [disabled] core members and [caregiver] assistants. How the downward mobility thing impacts them. This is important because L'Arche is a window into the spiritual journey unlike any Christian church or community. It is a movement the world needs very badly. Despite the incredible diversity of the community, we can live together in relative peace and share our lives with one another. Downward mobility helps us become free in the best sense. Not free to do whatever we want, but free to be what God means us to be; to develop our talents, to develop our gifts in the service of others.

L'Arche is a great sign. The people of L'Arche are involved in a deep human mystery, and I find that attractive. It resonates within me – the meaning of life, why we are here. To see clearly that the things we have are transient, that they are not our identity. Our identity is what we do right now and how we live. A good metaphor for L'Arche and downward mobility is the decision to become married; getting into a relationship with someone for the rest of your life. You never know for sure but you enter with hope. You value the relationship and the feelings shared between people. By themselves, the feelings are neither right nor wrong. It is what the couple *do* with the feelings – this is what's morally significant. It's the same in L'Arche. Downward mobility is about character in relationship.

Outside, the sun is new and brilliant. The freshly washed sidewalk reflects summer rain. Marilyn hails several core members from Robert's community. Tears are flowing freely. I overhear comments about the good man's personal motto – *Love first, talk later*. I am confounded by the veracity of compassionate love in Robert's life. His extravagance implores others to cherish relationship, sharing the journey for simple joy of another's presence.

A compassionate provocation

This book is about compassionate love and disability in L'Arche. The confluence of these bedfellows is startling, much like Marilyn's reflections on downward mobility. L'Arche considers itself a sign to contemporary culture. Its message upends durable Western ideals. For Marilyn, materialism and economic stability are poor benchmarks for lasting security. Democratic principles of individual rights and self-determination are unimportant next to affirmation of human worth in community. Fine German cars, fat retirement accounts, and courtroom justice offer flimsy support for authentic humanity. The L'Arche alternative is found in homes where others are respected and welcomed regardless of ability. Each residence is a place to grow and flourish in relationship. Human purpose is revealed for those willing to embrace the disability and suffering of others. In the practice of compassionate love, individuals befriend personal weakness and pain. Paradoxically, this invites liberation – enabling disabled core members and caregiver assistants to live with profound dignity.

L'Arche is extraordinary and mundane. It is culturally transformative and nearly invisible. L'Arche is a network of residences where people with disabilities share community with their caregivers. At first blush these individuals are relatively unremarkable. They get ready for work in the morning, shop at the market, and worship on Sundays. They catch colds and have arguments. Theirs is an earthy compassion, governed by a written charter which underscores the importance of relationships in community. Firmly planted in the Roman Catholic tradition, L'Arche is deeply religious, open, and tolerant. Core members and assistants are diverse, spanning many ethnicities and mental abilities. Core members are persons with Down's syndrome, schizophrenia, or head trauma. Caregiver assistants are newly minted college graduates, career lawyers, or recovering alcoholics. Some assistants have advanced degrees; others lack a high school diploma. Living with differences isn't easy. Much effort is expended toward everyday resolution of conflict. Many L'Arche communities exist on a financial shoestring. Caregiver assistants might receive a few hundred dollars per month for their efforts. Benefits are scant or non-existent. L'Arche flies beneath the radar. Its members are rarely newsworthy. Residences are examples of urban camouflage.

Yet these communities warrant a closer look. L'Arche celebrates people lavishly and with resolute sincerity. Robert is a fine example. Mentally about six years old, he was a giant among a cohort of individuals committed to the practice of compassion and love. While Robert did not lecture on love or write about its character, his actions commanded the attention of city government and religious authorities. He was exemplary even among his contemporaries. Robert loved abundantly and called upon others to do the same. L'Arche also nurtures people like Marilyn. Formerly a hospital administrator, she lives a downwardly mobile existence. Her reflections acknowledge the highest ideals of contemporary culture and respectfully shatter them. Disability means suffering, difference, and avoidance. None of these ideas are written into the constitutions governing Western nations. They are notably absent in popular media and speeches of political leaders. By encouraging members to acknowledge and welcome disability, L'Arche alters basic human definitions. The outcome is powerfully compassionate and unsettling – we are all disabled yet worthy of unqualified respect.

This is a novel mandate. What does it mean? Why would people give up security for a life of downward mobility? What sustains people to practice compassionate love in L'Arche for months, years, and even decades? How does disability matter to such questions? The following chapters explore these issues. The book compiles observations and interview narratives from a two-year study of American L'Arche communities. It is a work of ethnography, fueled by observations of compassionate love and disability unique to L'Arche. Ethnographies attempt to find answers through obser-

vations and stories. Ethnographic researchers typically live among participants for an extended time, often in distant lands with exotic cultures. But
this book isn't about the practices of faraway tribes. The subject matter
is defined by a social and religious movement rather than geography.
L'Arche is found in familiar places – Australia, Brazil, Canada, France,
Honduras, India, Ireland, Uganda, the United Kingdom, and the United
States.[3] Regardless of location, these communities speak a common love
'dialect' imbued with psychological and religious meaning. The book
attempts to understand this dialect through the experiences of people like
Robert and Marilyn. The language of love and disability challenges estab-
lished Western norms. It is a compassionate provocation.

My purpose in this chapter is to introduce L'Arche through the motif of
downward mobility. Brief comments regarding the origins and context of
the study make way for the narratives of several caregiver assistants. The
assistants are somewhat unusual for their longevity in L'Arche. All are
veterans with years or decades of compassionate service. Like Marilyn,
these individuals offer spontaneous insight on the matter of downward
mobility. Each narrative is followed by an observation of the caregiver
assistant with a core member in L'Arche. Compassionate love and disability are perhaps best illustrated where stories are enlivened by actual
relationships. The stories and observations suggest that downward
mobility is about finding a deeper humanity in others and self. The
chapter concludes with reflections on the nature of acceptance, respect,
and opportunity in relationship. The chapter bookend is a final narrative
which provides a horizon for understanding compassionate love and
disability in L'Arche.

Why this study?

Good ethnography demands a context, particularly given topics like
compassion, love, and disability. In 1999, a group of academics and
philanthropists met at the Massachusetts Institute of Technology (MIT).
Discussion points included human altruism and compassionate love.
These are explosively controversial in academic circles. For many scientists
they border on heresy. Studies of animal ecology and evolution indicate
that organisms behave in ways designed to maximize fecundity or ongoing
survival of the species. Those behaviors which appear 'altruistic' are never
selfless but reflect underlying mechanisms of exchange which promote
fecundity.[4] Auspiciously altruistic relationships between organisms are, in
actuality, a kind of symbiosis. From African savannah to Asian Himalaya

to oceanic trenches the biological message is, 'You scratch my back and I'll scratch yours.' Human behavior is no different. Concepts like altruism and compassionate love are religious or cultural ideals. What passes for these behaviors is stoked with self-interest. Regardless of appearances, the human story ends with the same refrain – competition and exclusion. At best our behavior is mutually empathic.[5] At worst it is selfishly deviant on the level of Rwandan genocide, Holocaust, and human slavery.

This may not be the final word, however. The MIT group observed that contemporary examples of altruism and compassionate love unavoidably persist. Mother Teresa's Missionaries of Charity is an example of compassion extended to the poorest, most destitute groups imaginable. The humanitarian legacy of Dame Cicely Saunders continues through modern hospice care for the terminally ill and dying. What evolutionary pay-off exists for persons willing to spend a life of chastity working with the lepers of Calcutta? What is the benefit for persons who offer compassion and relational intimacy to individuals who will perish in a fortnight? Is it possible that humans give generously without regard to personal interests?[6] Certainly these questions carry valuable moral currency. Altruism and compassionate love offer moral instruction for the school playground, corporate boardroom, and operating table. It might be worthwhile to consider options toward the scientific study of these issues. One of the philanthropic groups at the meeting, the Fetzer Institute, used dialogue proceedings to initiate a grant program on the scientific study of altruism and compassionate love. A request for proposals was issued in 2000. The present study was funded in 2001.

Prior to the grant award, L'Arche was unknown as an objective of social research. The movement is familiar in religious circles and among service organizations for the disabled. A number of books consider L'Arche on the basis of spiritual formation. Jean Vanier's writings integrate spirituality with insights on the philosophical and psychological contours of human nature. Henri J. M. Nouwen's many books on spiritual theology and disability remain popular more than a decade after his passing. These works quietly buttress the present study. Vanier and Nouwen offer moving examples of compassionate love in L'Arche, warning against reducing or deconstructing the issue. Laboratory methods might do violence to the integrity of compassion which spontaneously arises in L'Arche. Observational research avoids this danger while accommodating the diverse landscape of each residential community. L'Arche is a behavioral niche featuring interactions between persons of widely varied mental ability. Each community is different owing to the unique needs of its disabled core members. A representative account of compassionate love in L'Arche might well include observation of many communities rather than isolated cases.

As a result, the L'Arche project underlined participation and observation across a number of residences. Two guideposts were indicated. First, compassionate love should be understood through the perspectives of those who regularly practice it. Semi-structured interviews offer a forum for people to talk about what behavior means, why it is important, and what keeps them doing it. The broad spectrum of mental abilities in L'Arche makes it impossible to create standardized interview questions comprehensible to everyone. The project interview was consequently designed with caregiver assistants in mind. Second, the practice of compassionate love in L'Arche points to the example furnished by disabled core members like Robert. Observational research must therefore complement assistant interviews. The prominence of core members as practitioners of compassionate love makes it essential to balance interview narrative with observation. Together, these methods provide a useful vantage for downward mobility in action – an ecology of contemporary Samaritans.

With a nod toward the MIT symposium, the present research affirms the possibility of compassionate love as a matter of psychological relevance. Because of L'Arche, it recognizes the centrality of religious values, beliefs, and commitments in the practice of love. As love and religion work together in these communities, the project makes no attempt to isolate compassionate behavior as a matter of scientific interest. This breaks with a popular scientific view that behavior is best known in the controlled environment of the laboratory. The present study proceeds from the belief that human beings interpret their world in order to construct meaning. Compassionate love is embedded within the religious interpretations and priorities of L'Arche. As a result, the research considers behavior in its interpretive context, a perspective known as 'hermeneutical realism'.[7] For the present study, compassionately loving behavior is framed by the interpretations of disabled core members and caregiver assistants within the L'Arche environment. Behavior and religion are inseparably woven into member interpretations. One cannot be readily understood without the other.[8]

The book is a first pass at the issues outlined at MIT – an effort to validate compassionate love in human behavior. The work does not resolve the sweeping evolutionary concerns identified by the altruism discussion group. Adopting a modest approach, the study explores the landscape of compassionate love and other virtues amenable to study using non-reductive approaches.[9] At the time of writing, interview data from the L'Arche project are undergoing a fresh wave of analyses courtesy of funding from the John Templeton Foundation. These include mathematical approaches to caregiver assistant narratives, attempting to identify virtue in stories describing the self. It is hoped that findings will establish a framework suitable for the developmental study of compassionate love and other virtues beginning in childhood. Such a framework might include special laboratory games evoking compassion with real people and recognition of virtue in human faces.

Ethnographic research must be conducted in a manner which protects the welfare of participants. This includes protection of participant identity. Maintaining participant confidentiality was a challenge in L'Arche. All research projects happen on a budget. Funding limitations for the present study made international travel impossible. Because of this constraint the research effort was limited to my country of residence, the United States. Perhaps surprisingly, American L'Arche communities are few and scattered. In spite of distance these communities frequently come together for retreats and other spiritual activities. As a result, American L'Arche communities are familiar to each other and their urban neighbors. Protecting the identities of core members and assistants required more than simple name changes. Participant interviews and observations are carefully modified to avoid identification. References to local settings, geography, surnames, disabilities, weather, and even gender are painstakingly altered in the interest of maintaining confidentiality.

These notes service the real treasure of L'Arche – insights from core members and assistants on the practice of compassionate love. The semi-structured interview includes several sections which correspond to issues driving the main study. This chapter documents narrative responses of caregiver assistants to a section dealing with self-understanding and motivation to participate in L'Arche. Questions are adapted from work by Daniel Hart at Rutgers University.[10] Hart's research is focused on the identity of persons known for morally outstanding commitments. Main questions are followed by probes which help participants expand their responses with stories and anecdotal illustrations. In an effort to illustrate the value of interview participation with observation, each narrative is followed by a snapshot of core member-assistant interaction. It turns out that downward mobility is not resurrected asceticism. The downwardly mobile manifest everyday compassion in a manner that is surprising, at times groundbreaking, and occasionally profound.

*   *   *

I'll invite you to think about yourself in specific terms. Each question will lead you to consider how you understand yourself in relation to others. There are no 'right' or 'wrong' answers to these questions. Feel free to share examples or stories that explain why you perceive yourself as you do, or what circumstances or relationships help you to arrive at your conclusions.

What kind of person are you? What are your goals?

How is this significant in your understanding of downward mobility?

*   *   *

Adele is 44 years old with vivid green eyes and high cheekbones. She is greatly loved and appreciated in this L'Arche community. Her years of service span every role within the movement. Adele currently serves as local director. Her hair is wavy and dyed a reddish brown. We are sitting in the dining room of a Catholic retreat center near her home. The L'Arche penchant for hospitality is directly contributing to my waistline. The table is covered with flowers and tea and homemade cupcakes adorned with cream-cheese icing. Adele seems amused by the interview preamble with its lengthy treatment of informed consent. She smiles broadly in response to the questions.

> I'm an open person and an honest person. I deeply desire to follow Jesus, that's my founding piece. I'm hugely nurtured by my family and the community – it's about deep relationships. My work has deep relationships. That is what's important to me. It reflects the simple truth that I want to live out of a deeper place in my life. I like to have fun. They have this saying in my former L'Arche house: *Live well, love much, laugh often.* [smiling] This is what we live for. My goal is to be a just person, someone who advocates the justice of Jesus. Someone who is humble enough to say sorry when I'm wrong. I can roll with the punches and go with a difficult situation, but if someone or something has pushed me over to the edge, it becomes a real passion for me.
>
> I'm usually pretty happy and tickled in my tummy about life, very content. I love life. I love myself. I love the people in my life. My life is so full. I'm grateful to God for what's in my life and who's in my life. I'm very blessed. I volunteer a lot. I'm on the pastoral council in the parish. I'm the social justice person; have been for years. In addition

to L'Arche I do hospice work [care for the terminally ill]. I feel the same way when I'm with someone who is dying as when I'm with the core members. I also lived on a reservation with Indians, I feel that way with my native friends. The spirit of discernment is central to how I live my life – what does God mean for us to understand in this situation? I once spent a week with Elisabeth Kübler-Ross; that was amazing.[11] She helped me understand that I'm really accepting of people. That has come out of L'Arche; I'm good at accepting others. Whoever is before us, they are the most important. I learned this from Latimer, a core member in our community. He's a special friend. Latimer accepts everyone. He loves me very deeply, and I should love myself the same way. I've learned a lot from Latimer. Accepting, forgiving, fun-loving.

Some hours after the interview I am fortunate to encounter Adele with Latimer. The odds are against it. Adele's duties typically keep her away from the workaday community. It happens that Latimer's house is joining forces with another L'Arche residence for a movie night. Everyone gathers in the living room. Popcorn overflows several large bowls. The movie begins – a bawdy comedy featuring plenty of slapstick. Laughter is particularly loud from Latimer. With conviction he abruptly stands up, pauses the movie, and asks the group if they'd take a break to play charades. The consensus is affirmative. Seizing the initiative, Latimer pulls Adele in front of the group. Their theatrics loosely follow the minimal plot from the movie, duplicating the main character's acute gastro-intestinal distress. In the charade, Adele slips an exorbitant quantity of laxative into Latimer's drink. The house foundation shudders with a great roar of laughter. Adele laughs to tears and Latimer proudly bows to his audience. Then he wraps his arms tightly around Adele in an enormous bear hug. His behavior is instinctive, platonic, and utterly authentic.

*   *   *

Jason is 32 years old and completing his sixth year in L'Arche. He is tall with long brown hair pulled back into a ponytail. This style exposes prominent sideburns. He strikes an effective impression of late 1960s counter-culture. But Jason's measured speech is miles away from Northern California yurts. We are chatting inside an ancient barn on upturned bales of hay. The barn is located on a small farm owned by this L'Arche community. The farm is a place where core members and assistants come to work. Dragonflies hum in the air above our heads. The wind rustles through cornstalks and horses chuckle in the paddock. Jason is candid in his reflections on why he serves in L'Arche.

Most people would say I'm someone who does way too much. Tries to do everything else for everyone else and leaves myself behind. I'm OK with that. Some people say that I work too much and need to take time off. For me, that time off is working in the garden here on the farm. That's a way of alleviating stress. You come to a point where, sure, the money would be nice [grinning]. But it's still the dream job, being fortunate enough to work with the special population that we do, and also being fortunate enough to be the grower on the farm which I really enjoy. I'm the grower, that's the technical term. It's the fourth year I'm in that role. My dad, who was the program coordinator, finally retired. The marketing person was laid off because of budgeting and the grower also left. I took on the grower-marketer role for about a year and a half. We had a Jesuit volunteer [Catholic religious order] and she decided to stay on another year, and with her experience she was able to take on extra responsibilities, like working with the state, but you've got to draw the line somewhere. Five years ago I was a control freak. I needed everything done the right way; worried about the core members, worried that we weren't giving them the best care, that we were short-changing them. It made me an angry person. I've grown a lot since then. There's some highs and lows, a lot of introspection, you know, that Catholic guilt. It's a team effort and we should all work together. So now I come to meetings a little more calmly. I love to hear people talk. When I hear the assistants and core members talking it's really great. It happens spontaneously, like when we're out weeding. If we work hard today, we'll do other jobs tomorrow. Focus on the positive. We're here for them.

Later that morning the core members arrive. They come to the farm in small vans with several assistants. Jason greets each core member by name. Today's work involves harvesting beets. The beets grow in long lines at the west edge of the field. The hot summer sun quickly takes a toll on the harvest. Complaints fill the air. Jason brings water to the group in a plastic carafe secured on a wheelbarrow. He encourages the group to save big beets for a friendly competition. The largest beet will win a soft-serve ice cream cone from the local Dairy Queen. The pickers noticeably quicken their work. Sweat pours down necks and backs. Two hours later the job is done. Jason searches the beet pile for the largest specimen. Wanda is a core member with long blonde hair. She waves wildly from the furrow, entreating Jason to stop his search. She points to a final, unpicked beet. The top of the enormous vegetable is clearly visible above the soil. Wanda found a potential winner she saved for Jason. The young man carefully removes the plant. Wanda claps loudly, telling others to look. 'Jason found the biggest beet! Jason wins the ice cream cone! Jason is the best farmer in Kansas!' Applause erupts with prolonged enthusiasm. The entire crew departs for Dairy Queen. Jason drives the lead van. His smile is incandescent, filling the rearview mirror.

*   *   *

Duncan is 40. Originally from a Puerto Rican borough of New York City, he is crowned with salt-and-pepper curls. His eyeglasses are narrow black ovals, giving him a look of cool intelligence. Duncan was once a corporate accountant with General Electric. He is partly through his fifth year as a caregiver assistant. We are sitting on the back steps of his L'Arche house, a rambling bungalow in upstate New York. Thunderstorms are building to the south-west. The air is heavy and quiet with anticipation. Faint rumbling is audible in the distance. Duncan recently went through a period of reflection over his future in L'Arche and the meaning of downward mobility.

I like people to be up front with you, so that's kind of how I am. I don't try to be real complicated. What you see is what you get. I really love being around people. I get pretty energized by that. I am in the middle of the introvert/extrovert thing because I also need to have my own self-nourishment and stuff. I am a patient person; it takes a lot to ruffle my feathers. I can also be very sensitive [smiling]. That can be good and bad. I love music, that's a big part of my life and always has been. I work in our workshop at L'Arche, and it's a great place because I love creative art work. The workshop has broadened my horizons. I love taking an idea and then trying to figure out some creative way to help this person within their limits. To help them do it in their own way – I really love that.

I am understanding more and more in L'Arche that sometimes you have got to let things be, just let the energy be what it is and not try to change it into something else. [long pause] One of the big goals for me right now is to pay attention to how I am feeling and where I am now. To be able to look back at where I have come from; I think that's a real key to figuring out what your vocation might be. It should come out of you naturally. L'Arche has been good for me because I am encouraged to do a lot of reflection and have retreat time. I was recently on a silent retreat for a week. Actually it was two months ago, but it's still resonating. It was really amazing. Just time to process everything that's happening and bring it all together and try to make some sense of it. Just listening. I read a book entitled *Let Your Life Speak*.[12] So, with L'Arche I am taking it one year at a time. I have committed to a fifth year.

I don't know what my path is going to be, but I think that I am open to letting it fall into place. I experience a lot of joy and gratefulness for sure, and I also experience a lot of sadness. Sometimes the downward mobility thing is a bittersweet feeling. It's part of being with these people, the L'Arche assistants and core members, part of getting to know people so well. Sometimes it's very raw and bittersweet. These people balance beauty with all the crap that they have lived and hold. Knowing each other so well can be really painful sometimes. *Raw* is a good word for it. The core members experience raw emotions; they can immediately feel sadness and joy within the same minute and it's authentic and it's real and it's out there. L'Arche is not always easy. [face darkens] Not just with relationships and people, but, I mean, it's so chaotic. You can plan and plan and plan but there's always something that glitches the plan and things you can't plan for, so that definitely gets frustrating and exhausting after a while. But you also learn. You get to that tipping point and you think, 'Oh my gosh, I can't handle this any more.' But it's good too, because you have got to roll with the punches and adapt.

I only get a tiny feeling of what the core members must feel – of constantly letting go of caregiver assistants as they move on. [long pause] The interesting thing is, it doesn't get easier, it gets harder every time. It's harder to say goodbye and it's harder to welcome new people, but it is vital that people like me and others who have been here a long time are the most welcoming. There's this interesting tension that can be really hard. Every year in August is when my team changes, the workshop changes. I have a Jesuit volunteer and a Lutheran volunteer and this is when they finish the year and new ones come in and it's starting from scratch with new people. You build a lot together and then you have to work yourself up to welcome the new people and get excited. I mean it is really important how people are welcomed because it shades their experience of L'Arche.

It is evening on the same day. A meteorological tap is stuck wide open. Rain hammers the house with underhanded fury. Thunder rattles the windows like ordnance. No surprise, the electricity is out. The house is dimly lit with candles from the local L'Arche workshop. Several of the core members are anxious. Rennie paces up and down the hall, making soft whining noises. Cassandra is seated at the dining room table with arms clasped tightly around her shoulders. A new arrival in this community, she makes no noise or movement. From the living room I spot Duncan pulling a chair next to Cassandra. I cannot hear his soft words to her. But the effect is immediate and dramatic. Cassandra's countenance lifts as her posture unwinds. She begins to hum. The notes are audible even from this distance. Capitalizing on the moment, Duncan reaches into a pocket for his MP3 player. He unravels two ear buds from the unit. The buds are connected to a central cord in the form of a Y. Turning the player on, he gives one bud to Cassandra, helping position the tiny speaker in her right ear. Duncan places the remaining bud in his left ear. Eyes are closed as they listen to the same music.

*   *   *

Tamara is 29 years old. She is very short – less than 5 feet tall. Her blue eyes smile even when serious. Tamara lived much of her childhood in Africa where she excelled as an amateur gymnast. Her parents were involved in a Protestant development agency known as the Mennonite Central Committee. She is passionate about photography. We are talking in the main office of her L'Arche residence in the upper Midwest. Evidence of Tamara's hobby is everywhere in the room. Portraits of core members, wildflowers, and cityscapes are randomly distributed. Many of the pictures are black and white. Several times during the interview we are interrupted by core members. Tamara is tender and patient with each. Her touch is light, affirming, and respectfully bounded.

> I am a kind, compassionate, family person. I enjoy my alone time, like to be with people too. I like to do well at the things that I try, but I know that it takes me a long time to do well at them; it takes me a long time to get going. I want to get away from what other people think, but I am often influenced by what other people think, so I

don't like that about my personality. I don't think that I am concerned with money; I am thankful that my parents didn't emphasize
that in my life. But they are probably scared now because I am not
pursuing anything with money and my parents might worry about
security. But my parents have never really told me that, it is just my
intuition. It's a hard thing; money is always a hard thing. So, I am
thankful that I was raised by them and that they taught me their
values. They sought to live after what Jesus taught in the Gospels. Of
course they failed and we all fail, but they were very good at showing
that.

I think that is the kind of person I want to be, but I don't know if
that is the kind of person I necessarily am because it is hard to be that
way all the time. [grinning ruefully] I take a ton of pictures as you have
probably noticed, but I didn't have a camera for the past three or four
years, so I've been on hiatus which was good for me, because I can be
kind of obsessive about it. I like to make things with the pictures and
do little artsy things with the pictures. I hate to call it scrap-booking,
but I guess it is scrap-booking. I haven't been doing that very much
lately, but I love it. Even though I appear to be happy a lot . . . people
think that I am happy all the time. [long pause] But in the past few
years I've recognized that I carry a layer of depression. I have been told
that I have a 'smiling depression'.

I have been away from the community for three months. I've been
able to get in touch with what bothers me. It helped not having to be
responsible for anybody or doing anything. Now I am more in tune
with what bugs me. I have less patience, which I don't like at all. I
think that moments of exquisite joy are few and far between, when
most people think they are there all the time. Wonderful moments
like that are really special and I consider them spiritual moments.
They are emotional but also spiritual. If I can feel that intense joy,
that's a spiritual gift. I don't get angry, which is kind of probably why I
have been depressed. I don't recognize when I am angry, things don't
really make me that mad. But that's a problem because everybody
does get angry, right? I don't express it through yelling or getting mad
at people or whatever. I keep it inside. I am more apt to express
positive emotions. I want to continue to live a life led by the gospel
which doesn't really give me a lot of concrete goals.

I have always thought I wanted to be married, but I don't know if
that can be a goal because it's also a spiritual thing. Maybe I am meant
to be married and maybe I am not. God will allow it when the time is

right, if it's right. But deep in my heart, I would like to be married. [smiling broadly] I don't have a whole lot of goals like accomplishing things, like worldly success. The whole athletic thing was a major part of my life, and I was able to accomplish a lot of things that I didn't expect, but it still left me empty. Downward mobility makes it hard for me to set goals for accomplishing things, like worldly things. I think it is much more satisfying and fulfilling if I see growth through an interpersonal relationship or growth through my inner being. It may be painful, but it is much more fulfilling and doesn't rely on anybody else's expectation of me – it is just something that I can see within myself.

My goal is to continue growing spiritually, emotionally, interpersonally in my relationships with others and learning to be a better steward. One thing that has been on my mind lately, learning to be a better steward of the earth and seeing the whole earth as God's creation, rather than just people. [sweeping gesture] I focus a lot on people, which is great, but I think that God has created this whole planet and universe, and I think a lot of us Christians tend to neglect that. Jesus came for a human message, but I think we have a responsibility to take care of the earth, so I guess that would be a goal of mine. I like to celebrate and have fun, but maybe do it in ways that are earth-friendly, even though some of me thinks, 'That is so granola!'

Three days pass after the interview. The weather turns very cold. Outings require layers of clothing. Heavy snowfall makes it difficult to get core members to work. Nellie is sick. She is a middle-aged core member living in Tamara's community. Her vomiting is painful and unpredictable. Lying on the couch, she is fitted with towels, water, and a large pot in the event she cannot reach the bathroom. These items are arranged on a tray next to the couch. The television is tuned to her favorite show. Coming from the kitchen, Tamara gently places a cold compress on Nellie's forehead. Without warning Nellie vomits directly into Tamara's face. The smell is appalling. Realizing what has happened, Nellie sobs while continuing to vomit, sputtering wrenching apologies. With calm dignity Tamara clears her face with a nearby towel. She shows no hint of revulsion. Despite the fact she will probably contract whatever virus is ravaging Nellie, her attention is directed toward the figure on the couch. Other assistants bring dampened towels to help with clean-up. When Nellie is done, Tamara helps her rise. The assistant's words are simple and unruffled. 'Don't worry about it, Nels. Let's get a shower. You'll feel better.'

*   *   *

18

Sriram is 36 years old, the youngest of many siblings. A native of the San Francisco Bay area, his family is from the Madras region of India. Handsome and dapper, Sriram trained for a career in civil engineering at a prestigious American university. His move to L'Arche was envisioned as a 12-month break from work. Eight years later, he continues as a caregiver assistant in this Midwestern community. We are conversing in the backyard on a stunning fall day. The sky is azure and utterly calm. Trees are lazily dropping leaves around us. The air smells faintly of wood smoke. Sriram speaks carefully but with marked enthusiasm.

I am relational, extremely kindhearted. I think I am pretty fun to be with. I live with a strong sense of my life and how I want to live it and to whom my life belongs. I live with a lot of confidence about my place in the world. This is because I am beloved and have been my whole life. Yes. Absolutely. A lot of people don't have that. I remember one of my friends saying, 'You are so unique – you just expect that people will love you because why wouldn't they?' A lot of who I am just comes down to being cherished my whole life. Having stable parents, knowing they are present for me. All of that kind of grew me into who I am today.

My goals are downward mobility. I want to be more compassionate, I want my life to touch people, I want to grow and understand what it means to be spiritual. I live with a really deep sense of contentment. I was once pretty achievement oriented, before I came to L'Arche. I never think about what I will do after L'Arche, really, because I am glad to be here. It is so much more than I ever imagined it would be. I would love to go back to school someday. I would love to learn more. Something different from engineering. I would do psychology or sociology or that sort of field. I think knowing more about what's going on inside my brain. I think a great goal in my life is to receive people as they are.

I am prone to using boxes when I think about other people. The gift of L'Arche is that I had some amazing, paradigm-shifting experiences where my boxes were demolished. I mean completely blown up. L'Arche is a place which pushes me out of my comfort zone. I feel that all the time. Every day is different. Labels don't tell you much about why people behave the way they do. It's better to put the labels aside and let things unfold without expectations.

Don't get me wrong. This isn't easy. I'm an introvert. I like to start my day on my own. Life in community is a challenge. I don't like to open my door and see everyone else right away. But I am grateful. I care a lot about our community. I have a deep love for people who are struggling. I think it's more that I need a sense of order. L'Arche has challenged me to let go of some of that, like structure and order. I'm the kind of person who needs the day planned out. Sometimes that attitude goes against the grain in L'Arche. Things don't work according to plan. But I'm learning to be OK with it. I've become pretty relaxed. 'Let's go out today!' It is morning and then morning ends up evening. I live pretty abundantly. I give of myself. That is one of the things I love the most about living in L'Arche, because I have more flexibility and more time. People will call and say, 'Hey, can you do this or could you drive this person?' I can do it. It is such joy to make somebody else's day or week.

It is the day after tomorrow, about three o'clock in the afternoon. Sriram ushers an elderly core member named Moses into the kitchen. At first I assume this is for medications or daily chores. To my surprise, they begin preparations for dinner. The evening meal is regularly served at six, meaning the intrepid cooks will have three hours for their work. I anticipate a feast. But the meal is simple and cooked in a single pot. Sriram's scheduling is entirely for Moses' benefit. The gentleman loves to cook, making each culinary move an act of reverence. By the wall clock it takes Moses more than half an hour to chop a single onion. Each piece is painstakingly crafted into cubes of incredible similarity. Moses chops with the precision of an industrial diamond cutter. He chats with Sriram, all the while slicing with movements which deviate by microns. Sriram is obviously enjoying himself. Meal preparation in this kitchen is entirely about the journey. Edible outcomes are something of a bonus. Moses is nervous about the gas-fired stove and simmering pot. Sriram moves directly behind Moses, placing his hands over those of the older man. Together they stir beef, onions, garlic, and vegetables in olive oil and red wine.

*   *   *

Eric is 33 years old. A second-generation Vietnamese American, he is from Southern California. He explains that L'Arche is a costly decision. In a culture which places a premium on respect for elders, Eric is a long way from the medical career anticipated by his parents. He doesn't interact with them much these days. We are interviewing in the basement of his

20

L'Arche community in the Pacific Northwest. Sharp noises come from the kitchen floor above, challenging our conversation. Eric nervously taps his right foot on the floor. Seeking familiarity, he grills me with questions about the study. Gradually he settles into the interview with earnest and thoughtful responses.

I am a stable person. I kind of go with the flow. Just the day-to-day stuff, not really very dramatic or anything like that. I have goals that are oriented to what I live, to my priorities. I want to make sure that I am having a prayerful life, a lot of thanksgiving for what I have been given. A lot around relationship, just meeting needs of people, balancing my life, doing things I enjoy, making sure I am aware of what I need to do. I have a commitment to community. What is my responsibility and what are my expectations to live up to? Usually, just to feel gratitude or peace.

I'm pretty thankful on most days. Downward mobility is about simplicity. Becoming really aware of what is simple about our life. I know not to make big plans or become too invested in how something should go because everything can change at any minute. In L'Arche, it is interesting to make it to the end of the evening, reflect on what happened and compare that to what I thought was going to happen. Like, 'Oh yeah, I didn't quite get back to this or whatever.' I am open to what is going to be given. I enjoy tending to the home and the needs of people.

Downward mobility is basic. We all have daily skill activities. Helping people get washed up, getting their teeth brushed, getting their breakfast ready, packing a lunch. They go out in the day until about three. So we drive people there, we pick them up. We deal with interactions in the van. Sometimes we have a little bit of tension with whoever had a busy morning. In the evening we prepare the meal and people take showers. We take time to pray each night. We work on goals. Each person has goals that they work on. Not necessarily every day. But every evening people are working on some kind of goals. Basic goals, like turning on the lights or closing the curtains or getting lunch ready for the next day or working on laundry or something.

Our lives are simple. We occasionally watch TV and listen to music. We sometimes do puzzles. Some of our people work on puzzle books. We are big into the hook rug [a kind of crochet] at our house so people do hook rugs. We are doing hook rugs for our community right now. During the week we don't go out much because there is a lot going on. Please understand me. L'Arche isn't complicated. It's just life. But it's life in a way that the world has forgotten or maybe never knew. It's a life focused on people and relationships. It's a life where love matters. It's a life where time has different meaning. Let's be together because we might not have the opportunity in the future. Let's have some fun.

Our interview is completed just before the community heads to the beach for a summer holiday. The forecast is for fine weather and mild temperatures. We pack our bags with towels, sunscreen, books – the usual beach detritus. Arriving at a location with safe currents, the group sets up shop. The breeze is a cool alternative to warm sand. Eric is down at the water's edge with several core members. Sandcastles are on the agenda. However, a rising tide brings frustration for artists whose masterworks are rapidly destroyed. A core member named Tobias calls for a different game. He wants to bury Eric in the sand. With only bare hands the group excavates a depression sufficient for a large ungulate. Eric gamely climbs into the hollow. The group covers him with a great mound of sand, leaving only head and feet exposed. A core member named Carrie perceives opportunity. She begins tickling Eric's toes. The outcome is predictable. Peals of laughter and screams are heard above the white noise of crashing surf. With Herculean effort Eric removes himself from the sand pile and begins chasing Carrie. Soon, a dozen community members pursue each other like orbiting hornets. The game stops when Carrie and Tobias together crush Eric with a spine-altering hug. Like a championship soccer team, others hurl themselves at the trio. The mob collapses onto itself, a riot fueled by tenderness and affirmation.

*   *   *

Downward mobility is the impetus to uphold relationships as paramount to the fullness of human experience. Despite noteworthy demonstrations of compassionate love, the downwardly mobile are matter-of-fact about their behavior. No one seems to acknowledge that their actions might be considered virtuous or unusually empathic. While assistants recognize the uniqueness of downward mobility relative to mainstream culture, the gift of compassionate love is largely assumed. This is because the unfortunate alternative includes community conflict or relational fracture based on prejudice. L'Arche recognizes that relationships in a mentally diverse environment must surmount perceived asymmetry or imbalance. Human beings easily perceive mental and physical disparities, creating categories to manage difference through pecking order. Disability is social perception as much as physical abnormality. It is no coincidence that downwardly mobile assistants are called to explore their shortcomings and invisible disabilities. This tempers categorization of difference. Robert, Wanda, and Moses may look and behave unexpectedly. But the many similarities shared with their caregiver assistants far outweigh any differences.

What are the monikers of compassionate relationship? The preceding narratives and observations point to *acceptance* as a significant element in one's ability to love compassionately. For caregiver assistants like Jason, this involves relinquishment of personal control over the farm and its workers. For others like Duncan and Tamara, acceptance grows through spiritual insight gained on special outings. Retreats are a common feature in L'Arche. Many assistants refer to these experiences as watershed moments of acceptance. Learning to accept one's warts, blemishes, and imperfections makes it easier to accept the same in others. Acceptance provides a threshold for *respect* as a critical expression of relationship. An important goal for assistants, respect significantly emerges through core member example. Wanda's decision intentionally to withhold her prize beet is motivated by respect. Wanda knows that validation of human worth importantly requires public affirmation. This affirmation must be sensitive, respectfully honoring the individual on his or her terms. Wanda understands that Jason takes great pride in his role as grower. She turns the tables on the competition by providing a tangible example of his success through a trophy vegetable. The real winner of the vegetable game is the community which creatively confers respect upon its members.

Compassionate love becomes radiant when life is shared at close range, encouraging spontaneous and reckless caring. Robert was an expert in this kind of platonic intimacy. Latimer, Adele, Eric and others carry the standard after his passing. Appropriate and consistent practice of relational intimacy is hugely important for their communities. By placing core members and assistants in the same house, L'Arche is enormously risky. When things go bad, they are very bad. However, positive potential more than justifies the risk. Love snowballs when individuals and community are certain of intrinsic respect. Spontaneous movie night charades and beach-front dog-piles intensify collective experience of relationship as positive, meaningful, and loving. Charades and dog-piles only happen when individuals feel safe, knowing that expectations are repositioned away from upwardly mobile priorities toward the celebration of each person's gifts as a unique contribution to the community. This is the deeper meaning of Tamara's self-understanding. It is the basis for Marilyn's presentation of L'Arche as a hopeful sign to a hurting world.

Compassionate relationships transform everyday circumstances into loving *opportunities* for downward mobility. Sriram's use of *time* with Moses is particularly surprising. For Westerners, time is a commodity. Time is money. Time must be carefully managed to maximize productivity. Our metaphors are replete with urgent efficiency in 'redeeming the time', 'saving time', or 'making good time'. These familiar phrases are relatively meaningless in Sriram's kitchen. Moses loves to cook. Armed with an intimate understanding of the old man's habits and limitations, Sriram plans dinner without a schedule. There is nothing linear about time in the preparation of this meal. With the exception of the observing scientist, everyone seems to understand that the exercise is concerned with matters more important even than food. True, the community needs dinner at the end of a long day. But everyone knows that pizza is an option if the recipe bombs. The first priority is relationship. Time serves Sriram's objective to be with Moses. Time is transformed from a commodity to an expression of love. Time becomes an opportunity to validate those quirks and preferences which make Moses uniquely human. Meal preparation celebrates Moses before palate. That dinner was served at precisely six o'clock is nearly incidental. That it was delicious further polishes a shining demonstration of relational intimacy.

The porcelain wingback

Today is Friday, one week after the funeral. I am packing for departure. After two weeks with Robert's community I am leaving for another L'Arche network in a neighboring state. My bathroom sundries are nowhere to be found. I turn for the community bathroom about 12 paces down the hall. I am certain my kit is forlorn on the counter next to the bathroom sink. Scrubbing noises echo down the hallway, accompanied by an overpowering smell of disinfectant. The bathroom door is ajar. My knock is met by Oneida, the director of this L'Arche community. Back from a recent fundraising trip, she's now on hands and knees working the old Victorian tub. Her graying hair is pulled back, and long yellow gloves reach almost to her elbows. Her clothes are randomly peppered with dried paint. I murmur apologies for the interruption, motioning to my sundry kit on the bathroom vanity. Oneida chuckles and starts a conversation, grandly inviting me to sit on the closed and newly cleaned toilet. She might just as easily offer an antique wingback chair in a formal living room. The good woman can talk. I am showered with questions about my visit. How did I find out about L'Arche? Were the interviews helpful? What did I think about the core members? Shifting on the porcelain, I combine observations with heartfelt gratitude for the opportunity to live with the community. She nods vigorously through my response. Her eyes twinkle as she opens her mouth to respond:

I suppose we aren't quite what you expected. You probably didn't expect to find the director cleaning a bathroom this afternoon. But this probably fits with the whole downward mobility thing. Your questions made me think again about why L'Arche is important to me. I'm earthy. I'm soul-searching about my life. I look for meaning. I'm an emotional person who feels deep joy and sometimes feels depression but can work through it. I'm affectionate. I laugh a lot. I get tickled by things. [grinning broadly] I laugh at my own hypocrisy and recognize I'm an ass. I try to be a companion for others. That is deep in me and has been for years. I have fewer career goals and more goals in the places where I need to become whole and the places where I need to live reconciliation and in places where I can be a vessel of God's love. People are important to me.

I love L'Arche. This feels like the right place for me to live out what I'm doing and what's important. Over the past years I've discovered what a privilege it is to announce God. In how I am and in what I say. Often in prayer I say, 'God, if you can, use me to share your word.' I love that. One aspect I notice is that things are given and then they're stripped. Being a leader in this community I find myself looking ahead. I hope that I'm doing what I need to do. I want to be ready if the point comes where I need to step aside as leader. If I need to scrub the toilets and cook, I'm ready. I want to be open to that desire. I want to live in an open-handed way. I have a tremendous sense of gratitude for my life. A huge part of my life is listening to people tell their stories and I have a lot of gratitude for that. I've had some hard things to work through in my life. But I feel really grateful for some of the worst things that have happened in my life because I feel like God is willing to be with me and helping something to come from that – a blessing. So I find myself praying in thanksgiving. Finding good in things I wouldn't ordinarily call good. I cry a lot when I'm praying.

If I get killed in a car accident the most important thing is that I want to leave as a blessing. I could say amen to my life. Simple things delight me. Today Veronica [core member] and I were making cookies together. I dropped some batter on the ground and ants began swarming it. We got a magnifying glass to look at the ants. I'm talking to people about stuff like that and I'm going outside and doing the cookie dough thing and I live wanting to give to others. I've had to learn how to let go, I can't have a lot of control over my work. L'Arche is wonderful for me because I am tempted to be a perfectionist. I've had to decide either you give it to God or you really can't worry about it. I like all kinds of people. I'm interested in people. Down at this level, face to face or elbow to elbow, life matters.

2

Faith by Candlelight

I would rather a man be a committed humanist than an uncommitted Christian.

(*Martin Luther King Jr*)[1]

Dinner is over. Mealtimes in L'Arche resemble a family gathering with laughter, conversation, and the occasional pregnant silence. The meal completed, people are restlessly shifting in their seats with anticipation. Table banter is replaced with a sudden hush. Oblivious, I collect dinnerware with the vague movements of a newcomer. A caregiver assistant named Stephen leans over and shakes his head, motioning that we are to move into the living room. The group leaves the table and purposefully heads down the hall. Disabled core members and caregiver assistants claim seats like a congregation staking pews in a country church. The living room wall is dominated by a lithographed painting of Jesus from the nineteenth century. Riding clouds and surrounded by angelic companions, he seems to leap out of the frame in bold relief. A small guitar stands upright in the corner next to a stack of worn and creased hymnals. The coffee table is badly distressed with cuts and scuff marks. A crack runs through the surface glass. In the middle of the table is a mauve candle of broad diameter on a hand-thrown clay plate. The candle smells faintly of roses. Stephen walks over to the candle and lights three wicks in its center. He indicates that I will sit in a wooden rocking chair, a place reserved for honored guests. While this is happening, another assistant is lending hymnals to those who can read. She reaches for the guitar but does not play.

The glowing candle is slowly passed around the circle. Each recipient is granted an opportunity to offer prayer, make requests, or spontaneously lead the group in songs of worship. Spoken words, noises, hand gestures, and sign language handle communication in nearly equal measure. Group prayers on behalf of individual requests are completed by a simple refrain:

27

'Lord, hear our prayer.' Enormous tears are running down the face of Madeleine, a woman with Down's syndrome who tenderly holds the candle in her lap. She painfully recounts the anguish of a broken friendship. Next to her an assistant speaks emotionally of his uncle's recent death from cancer. The candle travels on, stopping with Scully – a disabled gentleman who breaks into song with great enthusiasm. We cannot fathom his tune, nor can we follow the words. But his intentions are clear. In the candle Scully recognizes the presence of God. He is overcome with joy and gratitude. As the candle circles the group, light shines on features of its handler which reflect suffering and disability.

Later I am with Stephen in the kitchen. We are washing dishes and discussing the candle ritual. Community members come and go. An elderly core member named Amy sits quietly in the kitchen corner. She appears to be listening carefully. Stephen notices her and smiles. He tells a story about the candle during the illness and death of a beloved core member:

> One evening the candle came to me. I didn't know what to do with it. My mind was just empty. Then someone next to me read a scripture. They knew it was one of my favorites. It dawned on me that I should read the scriptures to Evelyn [dying core member]. At that point she was in bad shape. She would be sitting all day long in her room. The pain was awful. To help, I'd put my arm around her and tell stories or whatever, but the pain would come back. So, I figured that if the scripture gave me a moment of peace and distracted me enough to feel what I should be feeling, maybe the same would be true for Evelyn. I passed the candle without telling anyone what had happened for me. The next day I was reading the scriptures. I took one sentence, highlighted it, and then wrote it out on a card so I could have it on hand for Evelyn, hoping it would comfort her. You know, she talks about God all day. 'Oh, the Lord ain't too weak, is he? He knows about this.' She really loves God – she talks about him all the time. But sometimes she doesn't think God will help her; she has doubts just like we do. I would read the scripture from my card when she doubted. It changed her. She would say, 'I need you now, God. You can do it; you're the only one that can.'

The candle ritual helps Stephen practice compassionate love in the midst of disability and death. His story matches my perceptions of L'Arche as a Roman Catholic movement. Religion provides comfort and meaning to community members, contributing to an environment where love is treasured and modeled. In Stephen's account the candle invites a deeper spiritual reality through the difficult days prior to Evelyn's passing.

A better humanist

Just before bedtime, Stephen says something which rocks my boat. Along with the majority of other L'Arche caregiver assistants, it is my assumption that Stephen is a Catholic. Instead, he makes a joke about how L'Arche makes him 'a better humanist' by giving him faith in God. It turns out that Stephen grew up without any faith. Prior to L'Arche he considered the language of religion to be meaningless; a strange delusion for people seeking an intellectual crutch. He never thought about spiritual growth or process – things routinely incorporated into the most mundane aspects of community life. Today, matters are different. He freely uses religious language to describe his experiences. Stephen often references his life in terms of a spiritual journey. The candle ritual is changing his latitude.

Stephen tells me that L'Arche accepts anyone from any background, including people without belief. Community experience mirrors this diversity. Although L'Arche is Catholic in habit, each residence is religiously eclectic. New members may quickly resonate with community religious practices or might require months to adapt. A substantial minority of incoming assistants find religion an unfamiliar and potentially intimidating aspect of community life. Stephen is fairly typical of this group. Not all of these individuals embrace religious faith during their time in L'Arche. But some do. In Stephen's case, the candle ritual becomes a window into deeper religious understanding. I am struck by his comment that, in general, the candle ritual does not fracture the community. Instead, religion in L'Arche unites people with different backgrounds around loving objectives.

There is more. Diversity in L'Arche is importantly a matter of the mind. The living room group is much varied in terms of mental ability. Core members like Madeleine or Scully are mentally about four years of age. Caregiver assistants like Stephen turned down graduate school in favor of L'Arche. Yet somehow the candle ritual speaks to all.[2] This muddies my water as a researcher. Religious concepts are commonly understood to be symbolic. That is, they require the capacity for abstract thinking. On their own, Madeleine and Scully should not be able mentally to connect the candle with abstractions like healing and gratitude. But they do. To be more precise, they share in a group understanding which helps create and sustain these connections. For the living room community, the candle is a tangible object representing the presence of God. Even if Madeleine and Scully are unable to tell us about things like healing and gratitude, the candle makes their experience possible. The ritual cuts across mental ability, leveling the playing field for religious experience in community.[3]

My purpose in this chapter is to consider how religion in L'Arche brings people together around the practice of compassionate love. Religion is a fixture in L'Arche. The meaning of love is richly illustrated through religious experiences such as the candle ritual. The candle is a touchstone for meaning and problem solving. It can shape the lives of its handlers. Following Stephen's footsteps, we hear from L'Arche members about how this might work. A cluster of stories describes religious meaning and resolution of problems within these communities. This is followed with a second cache of stories which expands on Stephen's acknowledgement that religion can lead to change as personal growth. L'Arche members grow in their knowledge of God on the basis of time, place, and role. This is accompanied by a simple truth. Regardless of faith background or mental ability, core members and assistants are, before anything else, beloved of God. This knowledge is bedrock to the practice of compassionate love.

Aboard the navy ship

How might the candle ritual bring together people with such extraordinary differences? One answer comes from an unlikely location. Edwin Hutchins is a professor of anthropology and computer science at the University of California, San Diego. Hutchins is famous for a rather bold idea. He believes that groups create meaning and solve problems by focusing attention on physical objects or artifacts.[4] By pooling mental resources around artifacts, groups are able to make sense of difficult concepts or solve stubborn problems. The reason for this behavior is plain. On our own, we are limited in ability to make meaning or solve problems. Unable to keep everything in my head, I require artifacts like a shopping list when I travel to the grocery store. Tougher problems require artifacts enlisting the help of others. Consider the example of this page. The page contains meaning about religion, compassionate love, and candles. Words are put together to communicate meaning to the reader about these matters. But clarity doesn't come easily. I admit this page is not my first draft. The actual number of drafts is closer to 20. I require the expert assistance of friends and editor to ensure my intended meaning is clear. Good writing takes a village. The page is an artifact where I publicly work out meaning and solve problems which, up until the moment of writing, were dimly illuminated in my head.

Examples of Hutchins' insight are everywhere. Think about the most important object in a soccer game. The soccer ball is more than leather, rubber, and air. It is an artifact for an entire team of individuals; people who pool their mental and physical resources jointly to create meaning and solve problems. Prior to a game, the team captain might tell players the ball is about *trust, creativity, teamwork,* and *strategy.* These are deeply meaningful words. They are metaphors for life – a fact not lost on count-less fans who spend good money to watch soccer games. The captain's words indicate that the game requires group effort to overcome obstacles and problems. Every player knows that individuals, even talented stars, are rarely successful in moving the ball past defenders by themselves. In order to reach its goal, the ball requires a group of people willing to share resources. The ball must be passed from person to person, following a pathway established by many rather than one.

Perhaps unexpectedly, Hutchins' idea of pooled resources and artifacts comes from research conducted on the bridge of a navy warship entering the port of San Diego. The task of bringing a great ship into harbor requires six navigators working closely together. Each member is responsi-ble for a specific task. Some take depth soundings, others note visual land-marks, and still others monitor ship speed. The shared goal is a plotted course on a nautical chart. This course must safely bring the ship into its assigned berth without running aground or colliding with pleasure craft. Meaning contributed by each navigation team member must be assem-bled in a way that is clearly understood by the person who steers the ship. Relevant artifacts include things like binoculars, calculators, and com-passes. These are focused on the most important artifact in this situation, the nautical chart upon which a safe course is plotted.

Hutchins' work affronts an individualistic culture. Meaning and prob-lem solving are not confined to individuals. These readily move beyond boundaries of skin and skull. Aboard the navy ship, meaning and problem solving involve coordination between half a dozen navigators. At precisely determined moments, each navigator calls out depth soundings or ship speed to the head navigator. Ritualistic behavior of the crew, working closely with binoculars and calculators, focuses meaning con-firming the correct course for the ship. Some might question the logic of such an elaborate system. Isn't a single navigator able to bring the ship successfully into harbor? Evidently the United States Navy doesn't want to find out. Specially trained navigators aren't cheap. The navy makes a substantial commitment in placing six of these people on the bridge of a single ship. Even in a highly individualized and technologically advanced society, accommodations are made for individuals limited in ability to make meaning and solve problems.

The idea that artifacts serve as warehouses for meaning and problem solving is not new. Hutchins leans into the work of scientists from decades past. The Russian psychologist Vygotsky made a similar argument more than 70 years ago.[5] Watching children with toys, Vygotsky believed that all mental functions pass through a 'social' stage in development. This is the reason why children play with toys, build things with blocks, and talk to themselves. What we perceive as internal mental function is first realized in the external world of human relationships. As an example, a young girl might be told by an adult to share with peers. But the idea of sharing isn't fully understood or personalized by the child until she works it out in practice. Even before a trial with real peers, the child might play with dolls arguing over a piece of fruit or toy cars attempting to share an intentionally narrow road. Owing to the highly social character of human thought and behavior, children do not fully understand the notion of sharing until they externally touch and handle the concept in a relational way.

It is true that many miles separate the navy ship from the L'Arche living room. Hutchins' work is not primarily concerned with religious experience, compassionate love, or disability.[6] But similar principles of meaning and problem solving are visible in the candle ritual. As the candle travels around the circle, the artifact links religious meaning such as healing with the problematic anguish of Madeleine's broken friendship. The candle becomes a centerpiece in Stephen's search for divine comfort through the difficult time leading up to Evelyn's passing. For disabled core member and caregiver assistant, artifact (candle) and ritual (request for prayer, worship, insight) help assemble religious meaning in the face of real-world problems and difficulties, reminding the community of God's faithfulness. The navigational 'task' before L'Arche is to bridge religious meaning with contemporary problems and struggles which require God's intervention. Differences in religious background and mental ability are minimized when these pathways are collectively built around the candle.[7]

In a nutshell, the candle exemplifies the presence of God. It stands for love, joy, gratitude, forgiveness, reconciliation, healing and many other important religious concepts. Individuals are unable to recall all of these meanings in a given moment. Even a bright and academically accomplished individual like Stephen needs to be reminded of the candle and its many meanings. With movement around the circle perimeter, the candle evokes the collective memory of the group. As Madeleine hurts, someone reminds her that God can heal her pain. As Stephen's mind is blank, a neighbor reads scripture about how God comforts the desolate. The candle carries the religious story in L'Arche. Based on a past marked by God's faithfulness, the story is continually written and rewritten in light of contemporary problems facing the community.

Finding meaning, solving problems

The candle ritual is not magic. The living room group is not a cult. Its members do not engage in brainwashing. By itself, the candle lacks any real power. But in the L'Arche community it comes alive – endowed with meaning that points to God's presence. Following my experience with the candle ritual, I mentally highlighted the centrality of religious questions in my L'Arche interview. These questions sought to find out what kinds of religious meaning were understood within these communities. Additionally, I hoped to hear about the manner by which meaning helped members cope with problems and struggles. The questions assumed a central role for religion in L'Arche. But recognizing the many faces of religious background and experience in each community, the questions were framed simply and without reference to tradition. My desire was to avoid religious language, with the exception of 'God'. With this approach, I hoped individuals would freely share their understanding of religious meaning and struggle in L'Arche.

*   *   *

Feel free to share examples or stories that explain why you perceive yourself as you do, or what circumstances or relationships help you to arrive at your conclusions.

What kind of person are you with God? What does that mean in L'Arche?

*   *   *

Monica is 24 and single. She is a third-generation Chinese American, with long black hair and a winning smile. A recent university graduate, Monica is completing her first year as a caregiver assistant. Danny is sitting with us. He is a core member with rumpled clothes. We are outside at a wooden picnic table. The table is under a large birch tree in a narrow back yard. The Midwestern air coolly anticipates fall. Much like Stephen, Monica did not grow up with religious faith. Yet unlike Stephen, she considers herself an agnostic. Danny is fascinated by her responses, although limited verbal abilities make it difficult to understand what he is thinking. Monica is wry in her observations of religious practice in L'Arche.

L'Arche is Catholic, you know, but open to other faiths. Because of this, there is a lot of language that we have to work through. Very specific language. I didn't grow up with any faith tradition, and when I arrived, I was totally confused by the Mass. Where to sit down? What to wear? I didn't know what was going on. I mean, what the heck is a 'genuflect'? [Catholic practice of bending knee in reverence to God] I thought it was a kind of creature in the forest! [laughs] For me even the word 'God' is a language issue. I had to learn the language and I'm still not sure if it's mine. I'm working it out. The candle time after dinner can be a little strange for this reason. Others have made comments to me that God is some fairy godmother who lives in the sky. Some say that God is in our actions or our molecules. I'm an optimistic person and I think this world is the best thing possible. It can't get any better than this. In some ways I don't believe in the heaven language I've heard in L'Arche because there's amazing beauty in our actions. I believe our actions have consequences. I realize that this may be a Confucian idea that goes back to my upbringing. In L'Arche I've heard a language of heaven that says you don't have to do anything. Everything is perfect. Just sit and watch and enjoy. I don't know if this language has meaning for me. I don't think that's pleasure. Pleasure is consequence and knowing that you make a difference.

*   *   *

Adam is 32 and newly married. He is tall and thin, with a high brow and deeply freckled nose. Known by the nickname Jester, Adam is given to laughter and practical jokes. I have noticed that core members greatly enjoy and celebrate Adam in the community. An assistant for three years, he was raised in a devoutly Catholic home. With a smile he plays on his Irish heritage, adding an 'O' prefix to his narrative. In this way he recounts how he was taught to pray 'O'Rosary' and attend 'O'Parochial school' as a child. Our conversation unfolds at a local coffeehouse frequented by the L'Arche community. In this setting Adam feels we are less likely to be interrupted. He quickly becomes serious regarding the deeper meaning of religion in L'Arche.

> With God I'm a little kid most of the time. I'm playing like a kid. The only time I'm not playing is when I'm confessing. I think that in God's grace I'm a little kid. Last April I attended a L'Arche retreat. I was specifically told to 'hang onto the kid inside'. The retreat leaders saw me out on a field during a break. I was acting like I was six or seven years old. One of the leaders was a priest and I saw him walking toward me on the field. I thought I was in trouble! [laughter] Instead of getting mad the priest said, 'Hang on to that. Don't ever let that go if someone tells you to act like an adult. We need to act adult, but hang on to the little kid stuff.' I have always had that kid inside, but maybe it was inappropriate at times when I was using it. Hanging out with the core members, that's our thing. Some of the people in L'Arche have told me that I have a gift from God around the core members. The kid thing is the gift. What I'm trying to do is to polish up on that. I know I make mistakes and say things I shouldn't. There's a humorous part of being like a kid with God, oh I love that a lot. I have learned in the past couple of years not to put the joke on the core member, but to put the joke on myself. To act stupid or crazy or something, you know. That's how God works in L'Arche.

*   *   *

Zoe is 46 years old and divorced. She is from British Columbia – something she evidently wants to discuss after hearing I once lived in Vancouver. The pleasantries continue for a long time as Zoe becomes comfortable with the idea of an interview. We are on the back porch of her L'Arche residence in the Pacific Northwest. Unlike many L'Arche dwellings, this home is nearly new. A lovely garden stretches before us, with tall evergreens creating a verdant wall at the back of the property. Tomatoes are ripening in a large planter. Zoe was raised in a strict Catholic home. Although she attended Mass through the years, she notes that L'Arche is the place where she began to 'put it all together'. She smiles widely at my question.

> With God it used to be a constant battle. As a kid it was always like a big chess game, you know, God and the devil. A mythical chess game. [rolling eyes] I remember a Good Friday celebration in my parochial

school which was gloomy and gray. You're reading the Bible and getting into that downer mood. One of the nuns ridiculed me in front of the class, made me cry. Left me feeling like God was just waiting to pounce. Then I came to L'Arche. You come across people like Sister Janet and it changes your mind entirely. Or Sister Tanya who runs the food closet where many of our core members work. As a kid it always felt like a battle between me and God. [long pause] It's different now. I recently took a silent retreat for seven days. There's some stuff down deep that I let out, but I was afraid of it. Little by little I'm getting there. There's still a long way to go. God is in nature, in people. It's the goodness and love that people exude. With God I've become open and honest. My deepest feeling is gratitude. Over and over that's true in my spiritual journey, when I can reflect, it's just like that. Once in a while when I've gone through hard times and I haven't felt like God was there, I realize how often I overlook Jesus in my life. Many of us in L'Arche have been using something called the 'enneagram'. It's a way of understanding your personality and how God might use you. Anyway, I'm a six on the enneagram so I fear and worry a lot. But I have this idea that my religious life is like a river, and I can put my worries in a basket, and they'll go down the river of Jesus. I can pick them up further down the river in the morning.

*   *   *

Neil is 29 years old and single. He is a quiet individual with dark hair and thoughtful brown eyes. Although I have spent more than a week in his L'Arche community, this is our first extended conversation. We are seated on the front steps of his residence on a tree-lined street in an Eastern city. A neighbor slowly walks her Dalmatian past the house. Our conversation takes a turn when Neil asks whether, as a Presbyterian minister, I listen to confessions from people in the church. Quickly realizing how this might be taken, he informs me that he is curious rather than penitent! Neil describes himself as a nominal believer minimally experienced with organized religion. He is fascinated by things like the candle ritual. He thinks deeply about my question and speaks quickly in response.

I have my own free will and I can choose who I want to be. Some people feel like we are what we are no matter what happens. There is destiny and all that. But God expects us to treat everybody with respect and think about how we are all in touch with each other even if we do not necessarily know everyone on the planet. We are all on the same world and we have a lot of interaction, being in touch with nature and the people we see every day. I think God is everywhere. God is in all people, even if another person doesn't believe in God. I think that is something a person has a right to do and everyone is in a different place at a different time. It is not a cosmic lottery or Darwinian thing. I think our whole concept of linear time is very Western. I try to see things more as patterns and cycles that go around in a circle. The patterns have always been here and will be around for a lot longer. I have read in books or had conversations with brilliant, amazing people and have been granted the space to not only soak that in, but in L'Arche to apply it to everyday life. I definitely had to get it wrong a few times; stepped on toes and cleaned up a few mistakes of my own until I got to the place where I am now. It isn't easy. It never will be. But it is something more, I believe in it much more strongly. My uncle recently passed away from cancer. I went through a depression after it happened. Although it wouldn't have been my first choice, the candle time helped me put things in perspective. Even if you don't fully embrace the beliefs of the community, I think people are on the right track here.

*   *   *

Lynn is 36 years old and married to Ben, another L'Arche caregiver assistant. She is short, with brown hair and a fair complexion. We are in the family room of her L'Arche home. Core member Linda sits on the couch, wanting to assist me with the interview. Linda tactfully follows my questions with some of her own. Lynn describes herself as a 'wash and wear' individual. She and Ben live a simple life without much in the way of possessions. Deeply Catholic, Lynn comes from a large family in a blue-collar suburb of Indianapolis. Our conversation is frank and enjoyable. At several points she stops and informs me that the questions remind her of issues she once considered in therapy. She unconsciously thumbs a rosary while responding to my query about God and L'Arche.

I know in my heart that God is really free and wants me to be who I am. To freely embrace my identity as beloved. You know, the old tapes, the old compulsions, the old God images are totally inaccurate. L'Arche continues to teach me about this. I expect myself to always be loving and completely patient even when I badly need to learn better boundaries with very broken people. What I'm getting at is the issue of how I protect myself. I can get confused about what's mine and what belongs to other people. I keep trying to rescue or accept abuse. I'm the kind of person who probably accepts a lot of abuse in relationships. I have always tried to make things OK for other people. So I'm learning to detach from that. I'll give you an extreme example that happened not too long ago. A person was stalking me and I said to myself, 'Well, I need to accept it.' It feels really unloving to me, calling the police. The person was so broken and I know Jesus loves this person. Yet I need to take care of myself. There have been a couple of times when I was in danger. For a long time I was buying food and coffee for this homeless man outside the store. I finally recognized that he is a paranoid schizophrenic. I started to notice and realized that it is unsafe for me. I finally stopped doing it – that is a really hard thing for me to do. I have spent my whole life feeling responsible for every single homeless person I have ever seen. Like there's some part of me that feels that I should give it all away. I know it's connected to my family stuff. I can get confused around that stuff; trying to understand that I'm not Jesus and asking God, 'What should I do?'

*   *   *

Sarah is 64 years old. A veteran L'Arche caregiver assistant, she moved into the community following a divorce in her early forties. She is slowing down but still moves with characteristic flair and enthusiasm. Her bright blue eyes are framed by long white hair and deeply crinkled forehead. Sarah loves to set out formal tea, a habit dating back to childhood. We are in the kitchen enjoying a cup of Earl Grey and cookies known as Peek Freans. Sarah is an elder stateswoman in L'Arche. Once community director, she decided her best calling is to live with core members. For Sarah religious meaning comes from faith referred to as 'a long obedience'. Her reflections are colorful, fast-paced, and seasoned with honest struggle.

These days I'm all over the map with God. Sometimes I'm really angry with God. Other times I'm grateful – I can never figure out God. I guess this is why we have God and not somebody that we make for ourselves. So often I've thought to myself, 'I'm on the right track.' But then things will slide off. I can't quite figure God out. I'll tell you a story that comes from my time in L'Arche – actually just a few months ago. One of my friends has a daughter in ballet class. I was on my way to her house for lunch and I made a blind turn and got creamed by another car. I hit my head really hard on the ceiling, and the battery was wedged up in the car and leaking all over the place. If you can believe it, I drove to her house like that. I arrived OK, but my car was bad. I was so careful at that corner that I didn't feel any guilt about it. I did everything I possibly could, which is a good feeling, but it was hard. If the other car had hit me one second later it would have been at my side and I wouldn't be having tea with you today. I wanted everything to stop. There was a spiritual part of me that said, 'Just stop and listen.' One more second and I would have been seriously injured. The car didn't explode, I'm alive, this is pretty amazing. I called Natalie [the friend Sarah was going to visit] on my cell and she said, 'You sound calm.' And I was! In a funny, odd sort of way. You see, normally I'm high-strung. It would be pretty strange for me to be calm after an accident. We were getting ready for supper and Jeremy [Natalie's husband] came home from an outing with a friend; this friend is a wealthy man, a generous man. He's very God-centered. Always looking for ways to give back the graces he's received. As he came up to the house he noticed my broken car and asked Natalie about it. We told him the story, and that we had called the mainte-nance guy to see if there was any hope for it. This friend of Jeremy's says, 'Sarah, don't spend any money on the car. Don't worry about insurance. I'll get you a new car and it won't cost you a penny.' I couldn't believe it – I knew that my car was on its last legs. I have very little money to replace it. I didn't know what I'd do. This man's offer was an unexpected gift. I think God is looking after me. I don't usually trust that these things will happen. I read about these things and think they only happen to Protestants! I always see these stories; they're usually tear-jerkers. I used to ask the question, 'Why doesn't stuff like that happen in my life?' Apparently now it does.

*   *   *

The stories offer two complementary perspectives on the matter of reli-gious meaning and struggle in L'Arche. One perspective is illustrated through the stories of Monica and Neil, individuals who do not identify themselves as people of faith. In a religious place like L'Arche we would expect these people to be treated as outsiders. At the very least, we might anticipate that they would feel relegated to the community sideline. Yet they do not feel this way at all. Monica is agnostic, but willingly attempts to understand religious meaning and struggle in the community. Neil is similarly attentive. Perhaps surprisingly, their efforts are not the result of a personal spiritual quest or desire to become religious. They are attracted to L'Arche as a matter of service. Their stories suggest tremendous respect for the community with its explicitly Catholic meanings and struggles. They indicate that this respect is mirrored back to them by the community. L'Arche respects those who do not believe or practice in the Catholic way. Monica and Neil indicate that religious meaning in L'Arche is, before everything else, respectful of others. Details regarding heaven, God, and nature might at times be discussed within the community, sometimes with fervor. But the commitment is to respectful exchange. This commitment prioritizes relationships as the foremost concern. People are more important than dogma. Love reigns over cosmic details.

A second perspective is evident through the stories of Adam, Zoe, Lynn, and Sarah. These are people of religious faith and background. They offer insight regarding the specific meaning of religion in L'Arche. God loves childlike attitudes and behaviors. God perceives our fears and worries, releasing us from their burden. God promotes freedom from past insecurities and shortcomings. God is attentive to needs, sometimes intervening in spectacular fashion. The God of L'Arche is interested in things like jokes, worries, personal safety, and broken automobiles. Religious meaning is directly related to real-world problems and struggles. It is further related to 'solutions' in the affirmation of all as beloved or worthy of love. Adam learns that he can brighten the day of core members when a joke is shared rather than made at another's expense. Zoe discovers that she does not have to shoulder her worries alone. Lynn understands that she can share God's love for others when she first honors herself. Sarah's broken car is replaced through events culminating in conviction of God's intimate concern for her welfare. Even though Neil does not identify himself as a person of belief in the tradition of L'Arche, he is helped by religious meaning in the candle to work through grief following his uncle's death. All of these individuals share religious meaning in the context of struggle. Tangible growth and renewal are outcomes. For many core members and assistants, exchange between meaning and problem solving is understood as a spiritual journey. This path is both individual and shared with the L'Arche community.

Growing and changing

Over and over again, L'Arche members made observations to the effect that religious meaning and struggle are connected with personal growth. Remarkably, no expectations are made by the community regarding the growth outcome. L'Arche communities are sufficiently committed to the worth of each individual that Stephen and Monica are granted space to walk their path without judgement or having to adopt the faith of the community. The journey is everything. If Stephen, Monica, and Neil choose to embrace belief – fine. If they choose to reject it, they are still affirmed, loved, and celebrated in exactly the same way. Compassionate love does not judge. Rather, it aims to empower each person to move deeper into the recesses of existential yearnings and religious questions. Stephen describes this as a religious 'invitation'. The invitation is not to conversion but toward wholeness. Granted, growth toward wholeness and healing is understood by L'Arche in explicitly Christian ways. But the growth process is as deeply respected as the people who walk the path. My second question on the matter of religious experience attempted to unearth the details of this journey.

*   *   *

What kind of person does God wish you to become? What does that mean in L'Arche?

*   *   *

Claudia is 56 years old. She is a French nun who began her L'Arche experience in Trosly-Breuil, a country village north of Paris. Trosly-Breuil is the birthplace of L'Arche. Claudia speaks excellent English, choosing her words with slow deliberation. We are seated in the dining room of her L'Arche residence in the Midwest. Claudia exemplifies Old World hospitality. Despite my reassurances, she is mortified that I am currently sleeping in the basement while the guest room is under renovation. Claudia warms to the topic of religious experience in L'Arche. In response to my question, she shares a moment of insight attained while recently walking a beach on Lake Michigan.

I am becoming a more vulnerable person when I am with God. This touches on my image of God, too. I find God in each of my relationships with people and in my relationship with the world and nature. So, I feel like a lot of who I am with God is the same as who I am with the core members or whoever. I try to be as honest as I can in all my relationships. It is not always easy. Sometimes I would rather keep the peace, especially with the hard stuff that needs to come up. That is a place where I really need to ask for help and support. I think that vulnerability is a major piece of my development. Being vulnerable when I am in prayer and quiet with God. Being as weak as I need to be or as I am at that moment. The idea of being beloved will require a lifetime to understand. Just trying to get my head around that. I know it is true on some sort of deep level.

*   *   *

Darius is 27 years old. He is from a large Eastern city. At Darius's request, we have taken the recorder and a basketball to a neighborhood park. The park is down the street from his L'Arche home in the upper Midwest. Darius is an avid basketball fan and welcomes any opportunity to improve his game. We shoot baskets for fifteen minutes before settling into the interview. Darius grew up with the fervor of a neighborhood Church of God in Christ, a denomination which played a significant role in the American civil rights movement. His three years in L'Arche cover a period of searching and reflection. Today he harbors more questions than confirmed beliefs or answers.

Things are really changing for me. In the past, not quite a year maybe, I have become more of an agnostic. I think September 11 had a little to do with that. I was in a space last year where I had some relationships that really took some hits. I don't know if that was kind of blaming God or whoever I thought God was or how God worked and so forth, but there was always a part of me that was more of an agnostic. When I first came to the community, I was of the mind that God was it. Before I came to L'Arche, I was looking at the possibility of becoming a pastor. But I think a lot of it was my upbringing. My mother is very religious. Most of the women in my family love God. In L'Arche I have come to realize what is authentically my own. A lot of what I practiced as my faith was what I had been handed, not things I embraced on my own. So I find myself now being more agnostic about

42

spiritual things. There was a movie I saw a couple years ago. It was a brother–sister relationship called *You Can Count on Me*. It was about this prodigal brother who comes back, but he is not very spiritual. His sister is spiritual, but her life is more of a mess than his. There is a scene in the movie where the sister asks a priest to come talk to her brother, to try to help him. The brother is basically resistant to this. He knows what his sister is trying to do. He says this thing that has really stuck with me. I am not sure if I am quoting it exactly, but he says something like this. 'I am not going to believe in something just because it makes me feel good.' I remember hearing this and thinking, 'Oh my gosh, that fits with me.' I don't know what the truth is. In terms of God and God's existence or how God works – there is a part of me that believes it might be a more beautiful world if there wasn't a God. Things would just be. But then there is a part of me that is deeply respectful of how other people view the world. If their spiritual-ity works for them, fine, but much of my agnosticism comes from my experience of religion growing up. There are lots of people in my family who tend to be pretty conservative and stuff. It can get judge-mental. Religion is something that they try to promote and get other people to participate in. That doesn't sit with me very well. Spiritual things are very personal and I have been in situations where I have had to be open about what I think my spirituality is and give a testi-mony at the school where I taught before coming to L'Arche. But at this point in my life I don't feel as comfortable with that way of expressing my faith. I am challenging a lot of the conventions that I had in the past and L'Arche kind of opened it up a little wider. I always questioned how the core members believed; what their sense of religion or God is and whether they sensed it was important. Is it important to have a sense of that? It seems like it is more important to simply be in relationship with other people.

*   *   *

Betsy is 39 years old and married to Tim, director of this L'Arche com-munity in the South. She is a former social worker who entered L'Arche after her mother's death from Alzheimer's. As we sit down in the living room, a core member named Dora settles next to Betsy. Without missing a beat in the conversation, Betsy reaches over and gently scratches Dora's back. Clearly this is something Betsy does regularly for Dora. After a few moments of this, Dora waves her hand in the air to interrupt. With tremendous gravity she informs me that I am interviewing the greatest human being on planet Earth. Dora questions me accordingly. Is the recorder working properly? Am I taking notes? Betsy smiles and blushes through it all.

When I really stop and look at my relationship with God I don't think that there's any more judgement than in my relationship with my best friend. But I often feel like I am disappointing God. I don't know if it's because it takes me so long to learn from my mistakes or because I am not really sure what I am supposed to be doing year by year, trying to figure out what I am supposed to be doing. It keeps changing. [gesturing with broad, sweeping hand motions] It's hard to tell. 'Is this really what I am supposed to be doing with my life?' Or is it more like, 'I thought this would be fun, but I'm not really listening to God.' For the most part, I know that God is not disappointed with me. Even if I am not doing exactly what I am supposed to be doing, God's not disappointed with me. I don't know if part of it is really about my own transposed disappointments. Right now, part of it is hard because over the last two years in L'Arche I allowed a lot of distance to creep into the relationship. I am not doing a lot of things that have helped build my relationship with God or even maintain it. I think that gets into the drinking water. I feel the disappointment because I haven't upheld my side. God is a lot harder to know than I originally thought.

*   *   *

Paula is 38 years old, with a warm smile and curly hair down to her shoulders. She is a Californian and relatively new to this community in a major American city. Prior to her arrival Paula was involved in the L'Arche Daybreak Community in Toronto, Canada. Paula speaks fondly of those years and her friendship with Henri J. M. Nouwen, renowned Catholic priest and author. Our conversation happens in the L'Arche home which hosted the candle ritual described at the beginning of the chapter. Paula knows Stephen and cared for Evelyn, the core member who shook the community with her recent passing. Paula did not grow up with religious practice, although she considers herself a Christian. She looks at the kitchen ceiling for some moments before answering my question.

I am learning to become at peace. My prayer life is not a list of petitions where I pray for things, even when Evelyn was sick. I prayed for Evelyn because it is part of a life that is about being grateful for what you have. I don't know if you ever read everything by the Benedictine monk David Steiner Ross, but he believes the most sincere form of prayer is any prayer of gratitude, so that is where I am even in the hardships. There is something to be learned from gratitude. This is actually part of the incarnation [the idea that God became human in Christ]. I don't want to go as far as to say I believe in a particular belief system. I believe in the consciousness continuing, the unconsciousness continuing; I feel like God, whatever goodness and compassion that God has in this world, comes through us. If we don't show it then we are not truly people of faith. I am talking about peace and calmness for others. This is the source of feeling that God is not a judge sitting up there with a pen to write down our many mistakes. God is not that person to me. Many people are driven by guilt or something else, but that is not where God lives. Let me go back to Jesus, let me go back to Jesus. When Jesus died on the cross, people talk about suffering. It was more than suffering; the cross was a great act of love and compassion. Parents do that all the time for their children. So my relationship with God is realized in compassion.
I think compassion and love means seeing the beauty in everything. It is right here and all we have to do is recognize it.

*   *   *

Johannes is 29 years old. He cuts an imposing figure with tall frame, square jaw, and hazel eyes. Johannes is a native of Franconia, a region in south-central Germany. He is completing his fourth year as a caregiver assistant in this L'Arche community. The son of a Lutheran pastor, Johannes refers to religion as the 'sandy beach' where he often played as a child. Emblazoned on the front of his T-shirt is an enormous black-and-white image of Mother Teresa. We are chatting in the basement of Johannes's residence in the Pacific Northwest. Water drips from a nearby pipe into a bucket, a rhythmic cadence aligned with his accented narrative. He speaks with polite authority.

I used to try to clean things up a lot before God. Things have changed for me since I came to L'Arche. Before, I was such a perfectionist. Whatever is going on, I would talk about it plainly to God just like I

45

would to anyone else. We have a very difficult core member named Roxy. Most of the time I could manage things well with Roxy. But sometimes I hit the wall. So I might start talking about it with God. 'Normally, I can love this woman, but right now I can't. You need to help me out with this. Tell me to act on what is most loving.' I will literally talk like that. I think it has to do with my being a perfectionist. This might be my habit because I suppress so many things around other people. Whatever the reasons, I am full of simple silent prayer. I'm more relaxed than I used to be with my faith. I love sitting in nature or in church and being with God. Sometimes my prayer is not what you'd call imaginative. But at other times it comes freely. I will be praying and Jesus will be at the campfire with me. The same thing holds true with distractions. It doesn't work for me to try and manipulate my life. Now I say, 'God, I know you are here all around me and I love you and I know you want me to receive your love.' So that's how I pray most often. If there are people I need to pray for, my favorite way to pray is meditation where I visualize the person. I'll see them in my mind. I'll see bands of lights wrapping them with light and that's God's love. I wrap them with God's love. I do this often for Roxy.

*   *   *

Holly is 34 years old and married to Jorge. Both are caregiver assistants in this L'Arche community. Two years ago the couple moved outside the community to begin a family. Holly found L'Arche through the writings of Vanier and Nouwen. Following the birth of their son Joseph, Holly spends less time in the community. Her narrative is tinged with regret about the transition. Her background is Southern Baptist. As we talk in the kitchen, a core member named Melvin joins us at the table. It turns out that Melvin and Holly are best friends. In response to my questions about God, Melvin excitedly asks Holly if she will tell stories about 'packages'. I quickly learn what this means.

I'm growing up in my faith. I'm learning that God wants me to spend time being and becoming. Not to make it happen on my own. I am always looking for something; I am restless, but I think God wants me to be myself, to live in his presence. That is what Robert [core member from Chapter 1] said, 'Be open to whatever packages God is going to send in the mail.' Right before his death he told me how excited he was to see his packages in heaven. Robert reminded me that God also has packages for me. He was so very excited about the packages of Jesus.

I finally believe that God really does love me. He laid out a 'rule' of love. The way to obey this rule is first to love yourself. You won't abide by God's rule if you don't love yourself. You must do it if you deeply love others. He expects me to follow the commandments and to love myself and others. I had better be careful here. I think in a way God is very demanding, but probably not the way you might think. It's not about him expecting me to get it all right. God makes a demand for me to love myself and love others. You hear about those conversions, you know. The born-again thing is an interesting phenomenon we all need to go through. But once you're there, it's not like, 'Oh, you made it.' That is just the beginning. God expects a lot from me and he expects me to talk to him and know that he is there. He expects me to recognize his creation when I see a tree or a mountain. I have a real aversion to scientists who make arrogant claims of truth. I have come up with my own saying. When a scientist discovers something, he often acts like he created it. He writes all these things about his discovery. But somebody else put it there! Don't forget God's rule of love. Don't forget to love others. Don't forget about the packages Jesus sends to us.

*   *   *

A friend and mentor once told me that growth happens on the basis of time, place, and role.[8] The spiritual journeys described in these stories are marked by transitions in time which happen in the safety of a particular place – L'Arche. With time, Darius is able to perceive his own convictions apart from church and family of origin. Paula gradually learns peace through the intentionality of gratitude. With these stories come hints about how time unfolds in L'Arche. Newcomers often comment that time passes differently in these communities; places devoid of concern for productivity and efficiency. Things march slowly to a different drum. Prayers are drawn out for no good reason other than the simple joy of shared experience with God. Meals can last for an hour or more. Getting a core member ready for the day might take the better part of a morning. Time helps members to understand religious meaning and make constructive links with struggle such that growth becomes a real possibility. The L'Arche community provides a place where this process is centrally affirmed in safety and with respect. The growth outcome is discovered in

Darius's revelation on the value of relationship. It is found in Holly's experience of God's presence through the packages of Jesus.

Member roles reflect community diversity in a way that is utterly inclusive. Leaders and followers exist in L'Arche, but these roles tend to work themselves out in a manner which minimizes status or pecking order. Accordingly, we find little discussion of God's role as divine judge or autocrat in L'Arche. Betsy observes that her relationship with God continues to push through disappointment. Her story frames spiritual journey as parent-child relationship first known by love and safety. Along these lines, Johannes is learning to put away the notion that God expects perfection. Claudia is growing into a more transparent and vulnerable faith. For these people, the spiritual journey reflects the L'Arche preference for roles emphasizing shared responsibility. More specifically, members understand themselves as God's children. With this role comes a quiet bombshell which informs the practice of compassionate love in these communities. First and foremost, L'Arche members understand themselves as the beloved of God.

Punchline

Several hours after our interview, I encounter Paula on the front porch of her L'Arche residence. I ask her about the word 'beloved'. This word is repeated again and again through interview responses to questions about God. Paula grins and wonders if I'd like to get a coffee at Starbucks. Together we walk through light rain to the familiar green storefront. Fortified with caffeine, we find a quiet table in the back. Paula tells a story.

> You've probably heard others say that Henri Nouwen was a spokesman for L'Arche. He was also a special person in my life. Not long before he passed away, he took a trip to California. At that point he was famous. He'd often travel and speak. Anyway, a big Protestant church asked him to come and speak to their congregation.[9] It's one of those huge churches with thousands of members. They made a videotape of Henri doing his thing. It was fantastic! I don't mean fantastic because of his speaking ability, although he does that well. It was fantastic because he said everything that I know and understand about what it means to be beloved in L'Arche. You can find a lot of it through his writings, but not always as clear as when he spoke at this church in California. Sometimes I'll watch the video just to remind me. When I'm having a bad day, or when I'm missing him.

The video starts with the head pastor of the church introducing Henri to the congregation. Henri is wearing his usual white robes. Then he begins to talk – big smile on his face. 'You and I are the beloved daughters and sons of God.' He says it slowly three times and then reminds everyone that this is the most profound truth we will ever know as Christian people. It's also the hardest truth to live by. The reasons are pretty obvious. If I remember right, there are three things that get in the way. [adopting Nouwen's thick Dutch accent] 'We are what we do. We are what other people say about us. We are what we have.' We spend most of our lives trying to live by these three things. I mean, think about it. In kindergarten they've got the kids talking about what they're going to be when they grow up, right? What are you going to do? It's all about your career. Then, we are addicted to the opinions of others. We feel great about ourselves when others say so, but not as much when we're alone. [smiling ruefully] We burn ourselves up trying to please others. Finally, there's the stuff we have. It's everywhere, on the TV and internet, trying to get us to feel good about ourselves in the right car or house or clothes.

So Henri is writing these three things down on a little dry erase board next to the pulpit. Then he gets dramatic. He loved to be dramatic. He attacks the board with his pen; he draws huge lines to cross out the three things that get in the way of being the beloved. While he crosses everything out, he says these three things are *lies*. They are the same lies the devil used to tempt Jesus. Remember? The devil tries to get Jesus to turn stones into bread, to *do* something that defines him. Satan takes Jesus above the temple and tries to get him to jump off so that God will rescue him and people will *say good things* about him. The devil shows Jesus the world and offers it to him saying, 'All this *stuff could be yours*.' But Jesus rejects these things because he'd rather live as God's beloved child.

'We are the beloved daughters and sons of God.' There's a lot that gets in the way. But in L'Arche we have a chance to find out what it means. We are finding out about God's love in the most profound ways and through the biggest hurts. [eyes shining] We are learning about what this means and how to do it with each other. Our core members show us every day. We show each other. Most of all, God shows us – and challenges us to believe it.[10]

*　　　*　　　*

Paula's story is the punchline to the candle ritual. The candle means many things, mainly the presence of God. But the candle is also an invitation to participate in this presence. The invitation is extended to beholder and community. Both are invited to adopt a new identity, before everything else, as *beloved daughters and sons of God*. This simple religious meaning reframes problems and struggle. It is the revelation in Madeleine's experience of healing following a broken relationship. It is the source of Scully's joy and gratitude. It is the comfort spoken to Stephen through scripture. The beloved participate in religion that respectfully discards the trappings of modern life in vocation, reputation, and possession. Rather than pursue these ends, the beloved are invited to discover their fundamental worth as human beings. This worth is most accessible when candle beholder and community embrace disability, suffering, and limitation. Belovedness is available regardless of religious belief or mental ability.

The chapter began with observation of the candle in helping the L'Arche community to understand religious meaning and solve problems. Based on Paula's story, we may take this a step further. As a core religious precept identified with the God of the candle, *belovedness* may do more than communicate healing, joy, or comfort. Belovedness unifies a religiously and mentally diverse group around God's faithfulness with the acknowledgement that others within the community should be treated as the beloved. Regardless of whether one believes in God, essential identification of self and other as beloved makes compassionate love the single most important priority in relationships. L'Arche members know that before religious background or mental ability, they are beloved. This fact is ratified by the group through meaning ascribed to the candle, but also through the manner by which core members and assistants strive to treat one another. Regardless of background or disability, the person before me is beloved. This is why an agnostic such as Monica chooses to learn the language of religious meaning in L'Arche. This is the reason for Darius's conclusion that relationships are centrally important. We may not share the same beliefs or mental abilities, but we share the same identity. Handle others with care, compassion, and love.

On several occasions I have shared these thoughts with my graduate students. One individual asked for a diagram to depict visually the candle ritual and its impact on the beloved of L'Arche. I have reproduced this diagram opposite (Figure 1). The diagram assumes group participation by a single individual such as Madeleine, Scully, or Stephen. While holding the candle artifact, internal mental functions are positioned on the 'inside' with external functions on the 'outside'. At the outside edge of the diagram is the candle ritual, complete with religious meanings discussed throughout the chapter. Interesting things are happening along the inside/outside dividing line for the person holding the candle. First, she or he *beholds* the candle as an artifact representing the presence of God. Second, the beholder *understands* specific meaning conferred by the group – healing for Madeleine, joy for Scully, or comfort for Stephen. Each of these is understood in relation to the beholder's identity as a beloved daughter or son of God. Finally, the beholder is *changed*. Change may occur in ways affiliated with time, as a matter of place, or with recognition of role. Regardless of belief or mental ability, the beloved are unified around the candle toward purposes larger than individual struggles or community conflict. L'Arche religion empowers self and other in the practice of love.

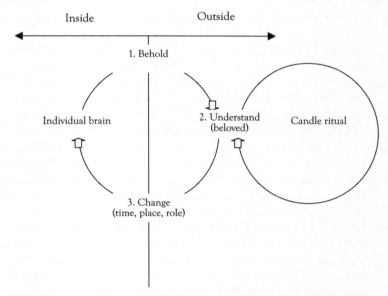

Figure 1: L'Arche candle ritual. Adapted from Hutchins (1995), Reimer (2005)

Listening to the beloved

I am rapidly descending stairs en route to a meeting with the director of this urban L'Arche community. Many of the members are away at work or shopping for dinner. Distracted by data and schedule, I absently reach the ground floor and fumble with the deadbolt on the door. I am partially deaf and hear nothing but the click of the bolt as the door is unlocked. Then it happens. I perceive movement in the living room at the edge of my peripheral vision. Tessa is sobbing. A core member with Down's syndrome, she holds her face tightly with both hands and rocks back and forth on the couch. At the same time, an elderly core member named Dominique is crossing the room with stiff, arthritic movements. Dominique walks to the coffee table, seizes the candle with gnarled hands, and slowly returns to the couch. She gently hands the candle to Tessa and begins to rub her back. Tessa uncovers her face and clasps the candle tightly. She beholds the candle as if receiving a gift of inestimable worth. Immediately she embraces Dominique. The tears have stopped. The entire interaction takes about thirty seconds.

I am startled to discover Neil waiting behind me on the stairs. He is respectfully observing the living room scene and my astonishment. Without a word, he opens the front door and motions me outside. He says nothing until we are on the sidewalk, safely out of earshot.

Paula told me about your coffee talk. About our being the beloved. You should know that Dominique teaches me a lot about being beloved. She is a Southern black, had a hard life, lost her babies still-born. She doesn't know all my goals, but she knows that I want to help her. She knows that I like to bullshit with her. She knows that I love her. She says that to me many times over. 'I know that you love me.' When I kiss her and rub my chin on her face, she says, 'Oh, you're the man.' She enjoys that. She just loves affection. Sometimes that is all you can give her. Listen, hold her, ruminate upon things a little bit, but eventually she will say, 'I know that you love me.' She is very insightful. She can't see very well now. But there is no hearing deficit. She listens to others. She waits to hear things and responds with love. If she hears someone crying, she's the first to care for them. She is really thinking about what is going on in the community. She knows she is beloved. She is teaching me that it doesn't take much to pass this on. I don't need eyesight or even to be smart. What matters is whether I'm listening – really understanding what love looks like.

3

The Transforming Moment

We live in a world of competition, where importance is given to success, a good salary, efficiency, distractions, and stimulations. Our world, however, needs to rediscover what is essential: Committed relationships, openness and the acceptance of weakness, a life of friendship and solidarity in and through the little things we can do. It is not a question of doing extraordinary things, but rather of doing ordinary things with love.

(Jean Vanier)[1]

Rain is falling as I make my way to the apartment door. A sharp knock is quickly answered and I enter to find a small living room. The interview participant is a diminutive woman of middle age with thick glasses perched low on her nose. In our pleasantries she is entirely ordinary, extending well-practiced courtesy. She reminds me of a librarian – warmly preoccupied in manner and business. Tea appears from the kitchen, a long-haired cat is curled on the couch, and rain quietly hisses against the windows. I move through my standard interview checklist, dutifully reviewing research goals and informed consent. We begin with open-ended questions regarding her personality. Not five minutes into the encounter, it is clear that I am sitting with an individual of remarkable capacity for compassionate love.[2] Through her years as a caregiver assistant to disabled core members, Katherine possesses an understanding of love in the broadest terms. Her reflections are earthy and pragmatic, forged through hundreds of encounters with the disabled. Mostly, her narrative underlines the central idea that compassionate love is first about core members and their example:

I'll tell you a turning point in terms of my understanding of God and L'Arche. I was seeing the gifts of the core members. When I got to Tampico things were rough and I had to live in the house because we were so short of assistants. It was very difficult. One of the core members was named Trent. He is blind and emotionally troubled. He was in an institution all his life, since a year old. I had this real love for Trent – a connection with him. I could calm him down, I enjoyed him. One night I was giving him his bath and I was drying off his back. He says, 'You're my friend, right?' I stopped for a minute. What occurred to me is how many people had bathed this man; complete strangers. How many people didn't see this sacred life in front of them, just wanted to get the job done. How many times he had to put up with that. What he's really saying is, 'Can I trust you? Are you safe? Are you my friend?' It occurred to me that this man probably lived through hell. Abuse. People being incredibly insensitive to him. Yet he can love. He can still trust. I could never ask somebody to be my friend. I realized that I was in a transforming moment, knowing that I'm more broken than Trent. I could not be this vulnerable. I thought that I was being authentic but realized he was teaching me something that I hadn't learned. God was really present in that moment. That is when I could say that I didn't choose L'Arche but L'Arche has chosen me. That's our spirituality.[3]

I have found that research interviews are occasionally disorienting for their profundity. Walking back to the car, my organizing beliefs about compassionate love are rolling over like a ship before a gale. Through the rain I can hear the voices of prized scientific and theological mentors from the past. There is my favorite undergraduate ecology professor discussing the 'problem' of altruism among orang-utans and bonobos. I hear the disdain in her voice as she responds to a student who wonders whether primates love without thought of receiving the same in kind. There is an esteemed seminary professor waving his hands wildly at the front of class, expounding on lofty ideals of love through devotional Christian writings. For Katherine, compassionate love is neither cold exchange nor rank sentimentality. Her transforming moment is all about Trent, a person with simple needs and deep hurts, just like the rest of us.

Are you my friend?

Katherine's view of compassionate love is unpretentious and workaday. It is a compassionate love of the evening bath, vomit in the living room, and badly soiled underwear. Not surprisingly, her reflections are about weakness and insecurity. Brokenness is the common thread that joins Katherine with Trent. In their recognition of brokenness, caregiver assistant and disabled core member are brought together to find hope in love experienced through relationship with God. This is patently counter-cultural. We hold brokenness and disability at arm's length, favoring celebrity images of strength and intelligence. We elect actors to political office, worship athletes, and purchase items endorsed by models. L'Arche is miles away from these values. For Katherine and Trent, trust grows where each comes clean regarding disfigurement and limitation. This trust is rocket fuel for the flourishing of compassionate love.

The kind of love described in Katherine's narrative does not call attention to itself. There is no attempt to interpret the encounter with Trent on the basis of moral calculus or self-righteousness. She doesn't bother to tell us why she found herself at Tampico, or why she chose to stay when conflict swept through the community. Neither does she appeal to triumphal, inspiring notions of love in the writings of others. Despite her religious faith, Katherine makes no mention of Christian theology. Her love grows without appeal to abstraction, pointing instead to God's actions revealed in the context of relationship with Trent. Her message carries a subtle warning to those of us interested in the study of compassionate love. If we are serious about understanding love that is fully representative of human experience, we should temper our reflections with the example of a former mental hospital inmate named Trent, a man who is cognitively about five years of age.

My encounter with Katherine was a personal watershed. Up until that moment, I had approached the topic of compassionate love in L'Arche with a kind of measured concern. I assumed that compassionate love invokes 'tit-for-tat' altruism, sprinkled with a desire to achieve inspired notions of care described in poetry and spiritual writings.[4] To put it baldly, we care for others because we expect good things in return and feel better aspiring to our highest goals and ideals. As I walked back to the car it was time to rethink the matter from scratch. Katherine's version of love was very different from my educated prejudice. Her love required little reasoning or planning to enact, seemed unconcerned with consequences, and was shockingly vulnerable. Far from the jungle or the theologian's desk, compassionate love involved relationships characterized by raw and elemental honesty. Compassionate love was about the other person who makes relationship possible, about security and trust liberating each individual to learn about the other more completely.

My purpose in this chapter is to consider love in the relationships of L'Arche caregiver assistants and disabled core members. I believe we have much to learn from the transforming moments of people like Katherine and Trent. The chapter tells the story of compassionate love through the narrative voices of L'Arche members. It is through these stories of need and growth that compassionate love is richly illustrated. Compassionate love narratives are followed with my own observations and interpretations. Months spent in L'Arche offered unique opportunities to know core members personally. My time with a core member named David and his caregiver assistant Sherry is a worthy anecdote to the remarkable vision of love that lives in these communities.

Love and Michelangelo

L'Arche is governed by a document that establishes relational guidelines and expectations. The *L'Arche Charter* points to the caregiver assistant–core member relationship as the first place where compassionate love is practiced and understood. After closely reviewing the charter, I wanted to develop a semi-structured interview that would major on how compassionate love arises in relationships between assistants and core members. This was a tricky business. First, because many core members in L'Arche are unable to speak, I would be forced to rely on assistants for consistent interview responses. As a consequence it might easily happen that interviews would favor the assistant side of the relationship. I had to develop interview questions that would to the greatest extent possible encourage assistants to put themselves in the shoes of core members with whom they enjoyed a close relationship. Second, I had to design questions about compassionate love that reflected knowledge of the L'Arche charter, but left things sufficiently open that assistants could share experiences without being led down a path of my own intentions. In other words, I had to anticipate the kind of love described in the charter but in an open-ended manner. It was imperative that the unique brand of compassionate love found in each relationship be allowed to speak on its own terms.

Both of these concerns required careful thought and planning. L'Arche is a religious network of communities. Compassionate love in the charter is known on the basis of each member's experience of their own beloved-ness. This is formally learned through Christian teachings including the words of Jesus, St Paul, and others. Given my twin anxieties outlined above, I needed a guiding principle for the interview that was deeply relational, considered the perspective of the other, and reflected basic Christian notions of love. Ethicist and theologian Don Browning offers a definition of compassionate love taken from both Roman Catholic and Protestant influences. Browning writes about compassionate love as self-sacrifice and having equal regard for others. This idea follows the example of Jesus, who consistently affirmed the basic human worth of others. For Browning, compassionate love arises in relationships characterized by mutual interest in the other.[5] Such love makes good psychological sense. From a psychological perspective, compassionate love means that one or both relational partners affirm valued traits in the other. There can be no more profound love for another person than that which recognizes the kind of person the other wants to become, and then helps that person to grow into their ideal. Armed with Browning, I had found a suitable starting point from which to design an interview for L'Arche caregiver assistants.

Social scientists are well advised to dig around in the research literature to find out if their ideas are original. Often they are not. As I searched the psychological literature on compassionate love and its relatives, I found a complement to Browning in the work of a reputable scholar. Stephen Drigotas and colleagues offer a theory capturing aspects of compassionate love sketched above.[6] Drigotas describes research with married couples who have experienced long and satisfying relationships. These couples demonstrate behaviors that enable partners to grow into their highest ideals. This happens through love *affirmation*. Put simply, affirmation describes how an individual is able to grow into her or his ideal through the efforts of a relationship partner to support the growth journey. The process of affirmation usually happens gradually for couples. Over time, each partner learns the other's unique characteristics and traits. Partners share this knowledge with the other, effectively helping individuals to know themselves more fully and completely than before. As individuals decide which of their personal traits are most desirable, growth begins. Armed with mutual knowledge of the other's ideals, each partner creates opportunities for desirable traits to be displayed, offering encouragement along the way.[7]

Drigotas and colleagues refer to their notion of compassionate love in terms of the Michelangelo phenomenon. The authors recall the artistic reflections of Michelangelo, who famously described sculpting in terms of the ability to free a hidden figure from the stone where she or he slept. This slumbering figure was an ideal form liberated through the touch of the artist. Drigotas and colleagues argue that this same sculpting process happens in couples who construct deeply meaningful and lasting relationships. Just like the artist, each partner sculpts the other into the other's ideal. The process can be described at two levels. First, *perceptual affirmation* suggests that the partner correctly perceives the other's ideal traits. Katherine and Trent perceive the other's goals in simple and often unconscious ways. Trent's ideal is concerned with worthiness for simple friendship. Katherine's ideal includes authenticity in her relationships. Through simple perceptions of other ideals, the relationship inaugurates new growth that was previously unattainable for each person on their own. In his vulnerability, Trent awakens Katherine to the possibility of movement toward her ideal through his example of authenticity. The cynical reader might point out that Trent may not be entirely conscious of Katherine's ideal traits. That is, he might not be mentally capable of perceiving and affirming her ideal traits in the manner described by Drigotas. But Katherine also seems somewhat unconscious of Trent's ideal, demonstrating great surprise at his request for friendship. Perceptual affirmation isn't much concerned with a conscious monitoring of others and their ideals. Compassionate love slowly and intuitively values the other, acting upon growing knowledge of the other's gifts.[8] Perceptual affirmation begins a loving process of sculpting the other such that her or his gifts mature and flourish.

The second aspect of Drigotas's vision of compassionate love is called *behavioral affirmation*. This describes how the relationship partner behaves in a manner helping the other move toward her or his ideal. Katherine's loving behavior brings out the best in Trent, leading to lifestyle changes that differ dramatically from his years in the institution. Conversely, Trent behaves in ways that affirm authenticity through honest admission of personal brokenness. Again, much of this behavior happens beneath the realm of conscious reasoning. How many baths took place before the transforming moment of Katherine's narrative? How many portraits of intimate, non-sexual encounter were required to make the Michelangelo phenomenon a real possibility for Trent and Katherine? There doesn't seem to be extensive deliberation involved for either person. No one is keeping score. The basis for Drigotas's theory, and for Katherine's and Trent's connection, is that compassionate love upholds trust and authenticity that prioritizes relationship above the interests of individuals.

Following Browning and Drigotas, I constructed interview questions to ask caregiver assistants about a core member with whom they enjoyed a deeply lasting and meaningful relationship. Questions were directed toward each individual's perception of the other's ideals (perceptual affirmation) and behavior designed to help the other grow into those ideals (behavioral affirmation). The main goal was to find out how compassionate love arises in assistant–core member relationships implied through the L'Arche charter. Looking at these relationships from the outside, it was easy to conclude that assistants routinely practice compassionate love in their care of core members. Less clear was the extent to which core members initiate compassionate love or effectively instruct assistants in its practice. As it turned out, the responses offered surprising evidence that my interview with Katherine was not unusual or exceptional. Core members regularly initiate compassionate love. In some instances they are expert practitioners.

*   *   *

In this section of the interview we'll focus on your relationship with a single core member. Stop and think for a moment about a core member with whom you have shared a special relationship. This could be someone you know now, or someone you've known in the past. Think about the bond that you share together and what makes (or made) the relationship so significant.

Perceptual affirmation
Question 1: Does/did your core member see you as the person you ideally would like to be?
Question 2: Does/did your core member regard you as the sort of person you would most like to become?
Question 3: Does/did your core member think you have the traits and dispositions you believe are most desirable?

*   *   *

Doug is 43 and single. He describes himself as a 'lifer' in L'Arche. A small man, Doug has large blue eyes and a receding hairline. We are sitting in a tiny basement office crammed with pieces of decaying furniture, including a battered desk festooned with pictures of core members at parties and gatherings. Doug is from the South, with an easy drawl and kindly demeanor. He apologizes for the crowded interview space. He offers a disclaimer to the effect that he is not a talker. Doug quickly disproves himself with insightful and sensitive commentary. He often refers to L'Arche as family. Alicia is his chosen core member, a woman in her forties. By L'Arche standards she is high-functioning, with good verbal capabilities. Alicia suffers from a traumatic brain injury. Her mood swings are severe and debilitating.

I lived at the house for five years. When Alicia had good days she would let me know about it and when she had bad days she'd make sure I was informed. [grins] I felt that there was love and respect no matter whether the day was good or bad. She could read me in tough times. She could sense and feel that I was hurting and she would respond to that. She could read me very well. She was the first person who could see me with my own eyes. If Alicia can read my body language then I guess other people can too. That was a revelation. Her unconditional love and acceptance of me was a revelation. It has been six years since I lived with Alicia. Every so often I see her at a yearly event. She comes up to me and taps me on the shoulder and says, 'Hey there little buddy.' Now you have to realize that Alicia is the *only* person I will *ever* allow to call me 'little buddy'. The consequences would not be good for anyone else. [laughs] But she says it with conviction and love that says I'm the only person she sees. It drops down the walls for me. Her actions, her thoughts, her deeds, and the way that she is a real person. I think a test of a relationship between two people is that you can try each other in tough times when the friendship is not comfortable. 'I like you even when things are difficult.' Alicia and I had that relationship. I've seen her get upset and yet the relationship hasn't changed. She's taken things out on me but it was OK because she trusts me and loves me enough to show me that dark side. Maybe that's why I've stopped spending so much energy to keep the dark side behind me. Because of Alicia I stop and realize what a relationship is. No matter what you are, no matter what you are thinking, Alicia sees those traits in me. No matter what has happened during the day she still comes up and says, 'I love you.' [eyes shining] She still comes up and pats me on the back and gives me a hug. There is a relationship . . . the trust starts when you share hurt. That was another revelation. I think maybe I am in a place where I can now look at some of my demons. The key is allowing me to be in a place of safety. When I'm hurting, Alicia can do this for me.

*   *   *

Nadia is 26 years old, of Mediterranean heritage. She is tall with jet-black hair and an arresting smile. Nadia is a turquoise aficionado. She wears silver earrings and necklaces adorned with the stone in a vaguely Navajo style. Nadia graduated *cum laude* from one of the top universities in the country. She greatly disappointed her cardiologist father when she left for

L'Arche. He expected her to pursue law or medicine in graduate school. The aftermath continues to make things difficult between Nadia and her family of origin. She brightens as she thinks about Elwood, a core member with Down's syndrome. Elwood is something of a legend in this community; an outgoing individual who deeply loved others. He passed away one year before our conversation.

Well, Elwood simply thought I was the best. I mean Elwood definitely had his most favorites and his least favorites, and definitely his favorites included the young pretty women! [laughs] So I was always very flattered that he would put me in that category. I felt like I was so beautiful and smart and wonderful whenever I was with him. I told this story at his wake; it was probably two and a half years ago. I was in one of the houses and the workshop is in the basement. I was having a really hard time with my life. My grandmother had just died and I had gotten really sick and passed out and broken my nose, so not only was I sick and throwing up but I ended up with two black eyes and my nose was really puffy. I was depressed and having a hard time in the community. With my grandmother and family stuff, I was really a mess. I didn't want to see anyone and I felt ugly and awful, inside and out. Outside I did look terrible and inside I felt terrible and I remember not wanting to see anyone and sneaking downstairs because I had to do laundry. In order to go downstairs I had to go through the workshop, and right then Elwood ran up to me and gave me a big hug and he goes, 'You're cute.' For that split second I forgot about my nose and my eyes and how terrible I felt, and he made me feel good. I would like to be that person, but I think that there's more underneath that it's important to keep close, and Elwood thought very much on the emotional level, which is important because I come from a background of academics and people who stifled their emotions and weren't affectionate. Intelligence and education were pretty much at the top of their list. Elwood didn't give a rip about any of that. Elwood was spiritual. Actually, he had a remarkable relationship with God. [long silence, misty eyes] For all of his suffering, he would sing and be happy and I want to be like that. I think Elwood rubbed off on me. I do think Elwood knew how much I loved him and cared for him, and he thought I was very special. I do think those things are really desirable, and I guess there's a little bit more too.

*   *   *

Chantelle is 29, an African American from the upper Midwest. She was a Division I volleyball star in college. Her long hair is straightened and pulled back into a ponytail. We are in the living room of a L'Arche residence, noisy with core members and caregiver assistants in transit. Chantelle wonders how she could have ended up so far away from home but insists there are no regrets. She is engaged to Antwan, another caregiver assistant from this community. The couple are seriously considering a move out of L'Arche. The weight of the decision surfaces in our interview, although Chantelle seems to lighten as the conversation progresses. Her core member is Robert, the deceased gentleman introduced in Chapter 1.

Well, I really want to say Robert but I will get emotional. I have thought a lot about my relationship with him. It's great to have someone always glad to see you. Even if I was getting rebuked by him, he would always say, 'You played volleyball, good for you.' Even then it was so obvious, he liked having me around, you know. I remember when I first came to L'Arche, particularly with Robert; I was blown away by his ability to show emotion from one moment to the next. He'd be laughing and singing songs and telling stories, talking about all these people he knows and then he'd be crying and he'd be talking about people he misses and different people who died in his life. So my immediate reaction when that would happen is to get him distracted and thinking about something else. But I don't think this was right. He was teaching me how tremendous it is to be in touch with how you feel. To be able to learn how to be with him in his happiness and joy and in his sadness and to be able to say, 'That must be really hard', and then let him cry when he feels like crying. To be able to cry myself. This was a huge lesson for me. You know, he was such a goofball. I tend to be a goofball and he was someone who really could bring that out in me. I could feel completely comfortable being as loony as I wanted to be and he would get a kick out of it, you know. I just felt completely in touch with myself when I was with him. I think he would challenge me. One time when I was helping him in the morning I remember him looking at me and saying, 'I need you, honey.' [weeping] I was thinking that I wasn't worthy of this man's total devotion and love – what have I done to deserve it? He really loved me. When he loved someone he loved them so well. You know, he would talk about me all the time; he would call me 'Tiwi'. So it challenged me to think, he does need me. But I need him equally as

much. It's not a one-way giving. I think something that really touched
me with him, and I have only recently been able to name it, is that he
loved so well but he received people's love so well, so he knew when
someone loved and needed him. We would just chat, you know. I can
be running around like a chicken with its head cut off and be forgetful
and get into flustered mode. He would be the one to make me sit
down and give me a blessing and make me stop. Or if I got to the end
of the day and realized that I hadn't sat with him and chatted at all, I
would feel it from him. I would miss it myself. So he always reminded
me of that, whether it was how I was acting or even what he was
saying, like, 'Where have you been? I was looking for you.' Constantly
calling me to come back.

*   *   *

Randall is 58 years old, of Polish ancestry with heavy eyebrows and thick
gray hair. He is married with several grown children scattered throughout
the Eastern United States. He is proud to show me pictures of his many
grandchildren. A bear of a man, Randall once studied at a Jesuit seminary
for the priesthood but changed direction after discovering Dorothy Day
and the Catholic Worker Movement. While serving overseas he met
Patricia, his wife of nearly 35 years. Randall's posture shifts as he reflects
on his relationship with Thomas, a core member whose practice of compassionate love was spiritually instructive. Thomas was born with mental
retardation that makes language difficult and self-expression frustrating.

Thomas. He is the one I'm most fond of. Oh my gosh, he is so utterly
sincere. Sincere love, sincere friendship. The kindness that goes
beyond anything I have ever experienced or come across or met or
anything you know. What I really admire about him is his relationship
with Jesus . . . I'll tell you a short story. It was Easter Sunday. We were
at the cathedral in Grove City. The church was packed and I was fairly
new in L'Arche and hardly knew anything, didn't know what he was
like. The other L'Arche assistants said, 'You're one-on-one with
Thomas.' They noticed that I'd connected with him and they trusted
me with him. So I said OK and we went down to church. This person
in the cathedral was kind enough to give us two seats on the very end.
The cathedral was packed with people. At the end of the Mass
Thomas was singing. I was told Thomas had difficulties with pronun-
ciation, so he was like 'ah, ah, ah' for a lot of words and you really

can't understand what he is saying unless you're around him often. So towards the end of the Mass, I'm trying to think of what song he's singing. Everyone is happy and joyous and all that. Here is Thomas singing 'Goodbye Jesus, goodbye Jesus' at the top of his lungs. I thought, 'Wow!' That totally impacted me. A few minutes later we bumped into the priest. We get out there and Thomas is blessing Father Buell just like a priest, 'Father, Son, and Holy Spirit.' He did it every Sunday regardless of whether it was Easter or Christmas or whatever. Absolutely beautiful. Thomas is kind and generous whether I'm seeing that from him towards me, or I'm not seeing that from him. There are still a lot of other things, spiritual things or kind things that he is showing me. The whole spectrum of what he is. Often this happens in a single word or gesture. I call it 'core member discipline'. It is amazing; he has this gift of saying certain things that make me feel guilty right off the bat. [smiles] For example, if I miss church he will say, 'Prayer next Sunday, prayer next Sunday.' Or middle of the week or towards the end of the week, he'll say, 'Church next Sunday, church next Sunday.' I'm thinking, how did you know that I didn't go to church last week?

*   *   *

Sister Joan is 46 years old. She lives as a nun in L'Arche, effectively breaking stereotypes for her vocation. Early in the interview Joan informs me that she is a 'spicy' personality. This appears to be accurate. She is dressed entirely in black, looking more Bohemian than Cistercian. Joan is curious about the research project, bombarding me with questions and making observations with short, incisive commentary. She is an opinionated advocate for L'Arche and the core members. Joan is graying at the temples, with a dark complexion she attributes to her Mexican mother. She warms to her discussion of Louise, a core member with no family.

Well, it is Louise. She lived with her family until about ten or eleven, I think they had a large family and the dad died and the mom couldn't care for the kids any more – they lived on a farm. So the kids got adopted out to relatives' homes and Louise went to an institution at that point, so she came to us when she was probably 63 or 64. I was the one who was involved in the process of finding a new core member for our community when Louise arrived. I went to the place where she was living and met her and was part of the decision to welcome her. I knew Louise from the beginning and lived with her at Naphtali House. When Louise came, all she could say was, 'You hit me, you steal my stuff, you call me names.' She didn't know how to communicate. She could speak but she didn't know how to communicate. She had never been listened to before. She would have all her stuff packed up in her room and all the posters down off the wall. She was ready to leave on a moment's notice. One night she was all worked up. When she became emotional, she would do housework. On this particular night she had the vacuum and it was ten o'clock in the evening and she was vacuuming in one spot. Over and over again, the same square yard of carpet. I came up the stairs and tried to tell her it was time to turn off the vacuum and go to bed. But she wasn't hearing that. I had to turn off the circuit breaker in the basement to get the vacuum to stop. I would wake her up in the morning and this stream of obscenities would come out of her mouth. It was not easy and there was another core member living next door to her at that point. He and Louise were like two firecrackers together. [grimaces] They got to the point of physical conflict and we were concerned about the well-being of people in their presence. Louise and I moved to a rental house and welcomed another core member. L'Arche talks about faithfulness in relationships that are built over time. Louise is a perfect example – one of those people who do not say much, but with the months and years we became closer. I use the metaphor of being in a car to describe our relationship. There is definitely a very special relationship with Louise. Our life together is like a road trip. She shows me the impatient side of myself, and then pulls me over to the side of the road and makes me slow down so that I can really experience relationship. Louise is one of three people in our community who doesn't have family. We are her only family. She does have a sister who visits her on birthdays and brings her presents at Christmas, but no, this is Louise's home. In fact, she is one of the reasons why I stayed in L'Arche. So she has slowly learned to talk. She is like a little kid who has taken in language her whole life and you know when she first came, she spoke words, then she put several words together, now she will speak in sentences. She welcomes everyone, and teaches us to pull the car over to the side of the road.

*　　*　　*

Michelle is 25 with brindle hair that changes color with the light. Right now she is dirty blonde in the setting Pacific sun. Michelle came to L'Arche after graduating from university. During her undergraduate years she heard about L'Arche through the local Newman Center, a Catholic movement ministering to academic communities. Michelle's Newman Center once hosted Jean Vanier as guest speaker. She is wistful recalling his charge for others to fully embrace their own disability by working with the poor. Michelle links Vanier's presentation with her knowledge of Raymond, an effusive and colorful personality. Ray passed away last Thanksgiving leaving a sizeable void in Michelle's heart and daily routine.

All I can say is yes. But it is not like Ray recognizes deep qualities in me all the time. There are other core members that recognize deep qualities in me and more often respond to those, whereas with Ray we just had fun together. Maybe that's why I appreciated Ray so much, because I am such a serious person and he brought out that side which is fun. He thought I was fun and he liked to dance with me and he liked to be spontaneous. I think a lot of people come to me and think I am super serious. So maybe that's why I chose to reflect on Raymond. Because he saw that side of me but he didn't dwell on it – he would go and just have fun with me. Yes, he let me break down my barriers of self-consciousness. We would go out to lunch and he would be so loud, laughing so loud or talking so loud that the whole restaurant would turn to look at him. You didn't understand what he was saying because he didn't articulate things real well. After he had some food in his body he could get so loud. It was unbelievable how loud. [broadly smiling] When I first started going out into the community with him four years ago, I was like, 'Oh my gosh, what's going on?' Then as time went on I thought, 'This is great. I don't even notice that people are looking at us.' He broke a lot of barriers, helped me overcome my own self-consciousness. He got me to dance when I am not a big dancer; he got me to dance in public places and got me to move slower, got me to really contemplate every move that I make. It took him a long time to eat and he made me really appreciate what I would eat. He made me focus because he did take so much longer, like I have a tendency to get excited by little things here and there. He reminded me that I need to focus and that to be present with somebody is one of the most special gifts, and I am not very good at it yet. He never made me feel like I was dumb or stupid or embarrassed or anything. He was never embarrassed by me. I often feel like people are embarrassed by me. So absolutely, he was a gem, I am sad that he is now gone. But I don't really feel like Ray is gone, because he is such a spirited person. I feel like he is here all the time, because I have gone through a few deaths with core members and I haven't felt quite the same about them. I mean maybe it is because he was so special and I missed the funeral and everything. I don't know, maybe I just haven't said goodbye yet and that's why I feel like he is still here.

*　　*　　*

Behavioral affirmation
Question 1: Does/did your core member treat you in a way that is close to the person you would ideally like to be?
Question 2: Does/did your core member help you to become what you ideally want to be?
Question 3: Does/did your core member behave as though you possess the traits that you believe are most desirable?

*　　*　　*

Mimi is 42 years old, of medium height with long brown hair. Her eyes are marked with laugh lines and a persistent twinkle. Mimi is completing her thirteenth year in L'Arche. Having served in every conceivable role for her community, she is a local historian with detailed knowledge of caregiver assistants, core members, and the challenges of keeping things financially solvent in an expensive city center. Mimi is enormously respected in her community. She warms to the topic of compassionate love and a favorite core member. Billy is in his early fifties and deaf from birth. Like many L'Arche core members, Billy was once institutionalized. Although he cannot speak, Billy has progressed tremendously since coming to the community.

We laugh a lot and he puts up with my mistakes. I most value being a person who is real. Not wearing masks. My core member is Billy and he's deaf. My sign language is getting better but it's not great. I can't be in sign classes all of the time and so I make a lot of mistakes and I have to ask him to repeat himself a lot. He's laughed at me sometimes, he'll get the giggles. Billy doesn't need perfection and that's a really liberating thing for me. Yes, because to be so loved and esteemed helps me not to take things for granted. Did you ever hear Dietrich

Bonhoeffer's quote, about how easy it is for us to use the poor for our own spiritual growth and edification?[9] I see the truth of Bonhoeffer a lot more. People come to L'Arche and have no idea how much they're using the core members. Outsiders who expect instant friendship. It happens all the time. People want to move in and have all the core members love them to death right away. Then they say they're going to write and they don't write. I could do that easily too. People don't do that consciously but L'Arche can be a place that makes us feel good about ourselves. Benevolent for being here. People say, 'Aren't you great?' For me, paying attention to Billy's love is not something to be taken lightly, for granted. It's a real privilege, a real gift. It costs me. He comes to me when he's upset or agitated. Or if he wants to be left alone. Billy's very clear. If you catch him first thing in the morning he says, 'Don't go near me.' [laughs] What I like is that we're good enough friends for it to be OK; if he wants interaction, or wants to be left alone, he's confident enough in our relationship to ask for it. I think we're pretty real with each other. He's been really angry; sometimes he's thrown huge tantrums, not at me but when I'm in the room. I think that's a gift. He can get so angry that he becomes frightened of his own emotions. Sometimes he'll let that out and he needs somebody to help calm him down and say, 'Stop it.' Then it's OK. I know that's a privilege. When he's really angry he doesn't ask for help in an appropriate way. He'll jump up and down; he'll never hurt anybody, but you have to look at him and say, 'Stop now. Stop.' For some reason that breaks it. 'You need to calm down now.' He'll do it, you know, it's like when I've wanted to throw a tantrum or have a big cry, to have somebody else be in charge. Billy will do that, he wants someone else to be emotionally in charge and tell him it's all OK. He doesn't do it much any more. It used to be years ago that would happen all the time. Now I can speak his language. There's so much of Billy's world that he can't communicate and he has such big emotions. I realize that I have a lot in common with Billy but because of people seeing me as strong, I've felt very lonely and isolated. With Billy there was a sense of communication that was much deeper. There's kind of a heart-to-heart level. A hug, a good cry on Billy's shoulder feels great. The complexity of things I think and feel I can't say to Billy most of the time, but he gets it. And I get him. He can really express himself. He's kind of paternal with me. We've taken turns, but he's paternal to me.

*　　*　　*

Andy is 41. An intrepid Scotsman, he lights up his surroundings with wry humor and witty anecdotes. He is married to Mimi. Andy loves philosophy and will gladly drop everything for tea and heady conversation. He is a long-term L'Arche assistant. Like Mimi, he has served in many community roles through the years. The interview is an occasion for reflection, a break from Andy's hectic routine. In particular, the topic of close relationship with a core member gives Andy pause. He is suddenly emotional as he reminisces about his friendship with Robert.

> He would accept anything, you know. Anything that was real, he would accept that. The thing with Robert is that I didn't have to go out and do anything amazingly grand. It didn't matter to him if I was going out and speaking about L'Arche. A lot of times I would do it with him, like we would go to classrooms together or something. You know, it was more important for him to sing than to talk about the history of L'Arche. I could have just been me without any goals or anything and that would be OK, you know, as long as we were spending time together. Yes, definitely, because I always want to be in touch with what I am feeling. I realize that, with Robert, I could talk about everything. I am sure he was always listening, but you know, sometimes he wouldn't really be paying attention to what I was saying or responding to what I was saying. But even so, I would be in touch with how I felt when I was sitting with Robert because he was so good at that. I would love to be like Robert. I remember, probably when I was 13 or something, we took this class about what we wanted to be when we grew up. They went around saying things like, 'I want to be a doctor', or 'I want to be this and this.' I said, 'I just want to be happy.' That was Robert. Despite his disability, his illnesses – he had to wear braces, he had to do a breather three times a day, three times a day he had to do this chest compression to break up the mucus in his lungs and he would sing through all of that – he was just happy and loving, totally connected with God. He prayed every day and sang and reminded people about Jesus. I would love to be like that. [long silence] He brought out a more loving side in me I think, when somebody really holds you. Any time you are with someone who really loves you and sees you as a great person you become more like the person they see in you. Robert brought that out. I mean it was hard. How could you be bitchy to a person who loves you and wants to be with you and thinks you are the best? You can't help but kind of become that ideal person. He brought good things out. Of course,

sometimes he wouldn't bring that out. Sometimes I would lose patience with him, but for the most part, no. If I was rushing around and he'd see me, he'd light up and want to hug me or something and you would just have to stop what you were doing, and he made you slow down. Not always, he wasn't a saint. I mean, he was remarkable and he had a lot of saintly characteristics. But he was also really stubborn and if he didn't like someone he was downright mean. He was both, he was really selfless and giving and generous but sometimes if he wanted it he would take it. Yes, he did possess some really wonderful and desirable traits but he had some other ones too. He thought I had wonderful traits; he treated me like I was great, he really thought I was great. I don't know, *desirable*, but I don't know that he wanted to be like me at all. Maybe that's what made him so great; he didn't want to be anyone else but himself.

*   *   *

Laura is 27 years old, petite, and newly married. Her curly brown hair is closely cropped. Her laugh is infectious. Laura and husband Shane make their home in L'Arche. Laura says that she fell into the work through Americorps, a national community service network. What was to be a brief sojourn in L'Arche grew into a long-term commitment and then a vocation. She views each transition with a sense of destiny. Laura is now 'house responsible', L'Arche terminology for community leader. Rosemary is her identified core member, an individual who struggles with bipolar disorder. She is mentally about seven years old.

Rosemary used to have a lot more manic episodes. She is bipolar and since we have moved back in, she has been in a more stable place. I think a lot of it had to do with her new work situation, having a calm place to go during the day. Often times when she came home from work she would be really angry and I think it was the stress. You know, it was a noisy environment with a lot of profoundly disabled people, sometimes loud and unpredictable and that doesn't sit well with Rose. It could be part of the ageing process where her body is slowing down. I think she knows that I am a person who is not going to get mad back at her. I knew that her anger was not about me or anything I had done to her. I let her have space. She could call me names and be pretty hurtful but it was never about you, just something that had happened to her. She has taught me a lot about being present to people. That is ideally what I want with my life. To have relationships where I can be fully present to people. [beaming] Rose has taught me what that means in a very non-traditional way. It is not about what I say to a person, or some great advice that I give to someone who is in a hard place. It is that daily faithfulness of just being with a person and being true to how I am feeling. If I can tell Rosemary that I'm having a bad day, she can put her hand on my shoulder and we really communicate something. Or if I'm having a great day and she is really sad we know that we can connect; we have a really honest relationship. We don't have to do it with words or great talks. It is all about presence. The accumulation of time together. In some core members there is a real instant openness and with some core members it takes a long time to get any kind of depth to the relationship. You can take one year or two years or longer than that to trust. With Rosemary it was definitely a slow progression and I do feel like she calls good stuff out of me and she is a delight. Joy in being in relationship with her. I think that she knew I was going to be there. They knew I would be getting lunch or a shower. Just those kind of daily things, cooking dinner and as my role has shifted it is probably more confusing for her than it is for me, I am in and out so much. When you are an assistant, you are planted in the house. You go out for errands and things. I feel like for all the core members here, having known me as a live-in assistant and now as a person who lives here but is not around all day, the transition is hard for them. Hard for me too. There are times when I want to be here to help and I know that is not my role. I need to let the team do that. I am the longest person in the house in terms of relationship with the folks because Shane was at the other house and the others are pretty new. Sometimes Rose is like, 'Where are you going now?' I know she trusts the other folks in the house and doesn't need me so much, but presence is something that connects us.

*   *   *

Annette is 35 years old. She is tall and very thin, with willowy hair and a prominent nose. We are sitting on the porch fronting an old Victorian home with six bedrooms. It is a hot summer afternoon in the Pacific Northwest and we are holding tall glasses of lemonade. The glasses are sweating. Annette is animated as she moves through the interview – a gifted storyteller. Her illustrations come fast and furious, as if she partici-pates in research interviews on a daily basis. Annette perceptibly slows as she reflects on compassionate love in her relationship with Mary, a high-functioning core member with a history of difficult relationships.

Mary treats me like a friend. She smiles at me when I come in. She recognizes me. She wants me to stay. There are little things that we do when we are together, where even if we haven't seen each other for six or eight months, she still remembers. She is really patient. She is supportive. I should tell you the whole story. We had been in France at L'Arche for some time. Just before I went home I was in a terrible car accident. There were three core members in the car with me and one of them died. Another was in a coma. The one who was in a coma was Mary. Not many people in the community really enjoyed her because she could get irritating. She was bossy and when you would tell her to do something she would do it her own way and she would get into a huff and get crazy. Kind of an intrusive person. When I had been there for a year, they asked me to move into her house. I was a little bit nervous about my relationship with her but I fell in love with her. She was amazing. She was strong and said what was on her mind. She had deep hurts that she was willing to share with me and I spent a lot of time with her, helping her work through different things that drove people crazy. I didn't mind. I taught her to work with her money more and I taught her how to use an ATM. I still remember the day that she did it by herself for the first time. I just sat in the car and watched and she came back with her card and her money and she was so excited. Not like it was a big deal, but I really, really enjoyed being with her. She allowed me an intimacy with her that she did not allow other people. She had old ratty bras because nobody wanted to help her try on new bras. We went shopping for new bras one day and it was really great. Because she was humble in knowing that she needed help – she had no idea how to buy a bra. She wasn't someone who needed any help with toileting or hygiene or anything and she allowed me into that kind of intimacy with her. So she was in a coma for two years and I, immediately after the accident, visited her every day for a week. I would have to drive past the place where the accident happened. I think it was shock and exhaustion associated with the accident. I got to the point where I couldn't see Mary any more. The realization of what had happened came crashing down on me. I was in France for two more months and I saw her three more times. Then I went home. I didn't know how sad I was until I left France. So I left France in August and came here in September. Went back to France

72

in April for a visit and couldn't bring myself to go visit her. I went
back in January and finally went to see her and she was still . . . I
think there are different stages of comas. She was opening her eyes,
but they weren't sure if she was actually recognizing anything. She
kind of followed people with her eyes. They let us spend about an
hour together. They had a psychologist with her because it was the
first time she was seeing me since the accident. We spent about half
an hour together and I just talked to her and said I was sorry and
cried. I told her what I was doing and I held her hand. She just stared
at me the whole time. [weeping softly] When I left, I bent my head
down to kiss her cheek and she turned her head towards me. She had
never done that before. Everyone gives her a kiss before they leave and
I gave her one and she turned her head towards me and they were
like, 'Wow!' So I did it again and she turned her head towards me and
I kissed her again and she did it three times. Ever since then, I have
gone all the way to France to visit her. The last time I went, I stayed
for three days, well past the end of visiting hours because they let me
and she just held my hand and stared at me. They told me that after
the first visit she started coming out of the coma and in June she was
trying to talk and was going through physical therapy. Moving her
arms and getting some mobility back in her hands. The whole time I
was there she just stared at me and I cried. She shook her head and
said, 'No.' When I asked her if she was tired, she would hold my hand
a little bit tighter. She remembers me. She puts her forehead up
against mine and rubs her nose up against mine. She won't do that
with anybody else. She remembers me. Even though I usually go five,
six, seven months between visits, she remembers me. When I went
and spent three days with her, I thought I'd have enough to talk about
for both of us for three days. Well, you plan for three days but you run
out in four hours. But that wasn't the point. She taught me how to be
with another person. That your presence is important. It's possible to
talk about anything and fill time; not really connect with a person. I
can tell you what the weather is like and what is going on in the
world, but she has really taught me how to be with people and know
that she doesn't expect anything other than being there with her.

*   *   *

The depth and range of compassionate love in assistant narratives is
remarkable. Not only do core members initiate compassionate love, they

affirm others at the deepest level of human understanding. Consistent with the many variations of disability in L'Arche, perceptual and behavioral affirmation happens in ways that reflect immediate surroundings, circumstances in residential communities, and particular relationships. It is probably unwise to harmonize or force these variations into a single love prescription. A better option is to note themes that offer wisdom on the origins and practice of compassionate love. Security and trust characterize the growth of authentic care, but with an understanding of *presence* that upholds relationship as the greatest value, beyond anything relational partners may accomplish individually or together. Transforming moments in L'Arche relationships are often marked by the realization that it is enough to simply be together. We don't need to do or achieve anything. Come be with me. Let me be with you. Compassionate love values the other at the expense of competing distractions.

With presence comes a different understanding of time and space. Caregiver assistants were unified in their insistence that knowledge and practice of love matures gradually. Spending time with core members means that dinner may be delayed. Shopping might be put off until tomorrow. As assistants spend time with core members they learn a new pattern of undertaking tasks. No longer is relationship dependent upon conversation or entertainment. Compassionate love is learned with intimate recognition that the other is where I find meaning. In this relationship I grow to realize that I am not alone; worthy of affirmation at the most basic level of conscious experience. The presence theme is a stark reminder that the world outside L'Arche is unfolding at breakneck speed, fueled by priorities of success and productivity. In L'Arche, time slows down and people shelve their ambitions, favoring the intimacy of a good joke or opportunity to hold another's hand.

What motivates people to value the company of others so highly?[10] The presence motif speaks to a deeper level of human need beneath compassionate love. Human beings are unique in the animal world for an ability to anticipate future consequences. The consequences we perceive are not limited to ourselves, meaning that we can extend our anticipation to include others. Our brains are good at remembering past experiences and even better at learning the signs of potentially traumatic or threatening situations yet to unfold. In particular, threats to our security occupy much implicit and conscious mental function.[11] Presence recognizes and affirms a central human requirement for security in the midst of uncertain and sometimes frightening circumstances. Presence is why family members will often go to great lengths to sit together on an airplane, entreating strangers to give up their seat in order to allow kin close proximity. Presence is the basis for hospice care to ensure that the dying will not perish alone. Presence explains why previously institutionalized core members are for the first time able to form coherent and lasting relationships in L'Arche. Presence is a central reason why caregivers are able to stay in L'Arche despite community conflict, misunderstanding, or financial stress. Presence recognizes that, no matter what our level of mental functioning, basic awareness comes with a price – that of uncertainty linked with potential threats to our security. We know that running away and hiding will not bankroll our safety. Things look different, however, in the presence of a trusted and loving companion. Presence understands this, helping the other move forward accordingly.

A second theme is perhaps even more striking, understood in *honesty*. Mimi's relationship with Billy is blindingly honest and transparent. Mimi and Billy might share a laugh, put up with the other's difficult moods, or ignore the other's mistakes. Compassionate love appears to help the relationship partner move toward her or his ideals. Yet there is more. Billy's love liberates Mimi not only for how he helps her to grow toward ideal traits, but where love *changes and reprioritizes those ideals*. With tremendous insight Mimi quotes Dietrich Bonhoeffer on the tendency of people to use core members for their own edification. She suggests that individuals are able selfishly to take advantage of core members as impersonal tools to help them grow toward an ideal that is grandiose and self-righteous. For Mimi, this is false love. Real freedom, she suggests, comes from Billy's love that demonstrates 'ideal' traits of an unanticipated nature, such as tantrums and emotions people are reluctant to share publicly with one another. Billy's honesty in these moments offers a reminder that she shares the same weaknesses, a familiar tune played first through Katherine's experiences with Trent. Compassionate love comes with Mimi's recognition that her ideal is to be authentic in a way that follows Billy's honest example. The price of authenticity is acknowledgement of brokenness, weakness, and fragility. Owning up to personal brokenness and disability separates genuine love from the narcissistic enhancement of those who use core members for their own ends.

Compassionate love in assistant narratives affirms the uncomfortable reality that we are all broken and disabled. Perhaps the greatest difference between assistants and core members is that the latter are less effective at hiding disabilities and hidden flaws. The preceding narratives suggest that assistants who honestly recognize their own disability are liberated from stone to discover new ideals made possible through compassionate love of the other. Billy loves in a manner that focuses Mimi's ideals from a vague interest in relational transparency to that which is most vulnerable, risky, and authentically human. For Billy, love is best understood when the chips are down, emotions are running high, and the potential for rejection is greatest. In Billy's world, compassionate love is an invitation to embrace those aspects of human experience that are apparently least worthy of equal regard or mutuality. In Mimi's view, the invitation is an extraordinary gift.

The puzzle prodigy

I am seated at a long table with a core member named David. We are in the dining room of his L'Arche home in the American West. The day is blisteringly hot and the room is without air conditioning. David is doing a puzzle. It is a ghastly affair with thousands of microscopic pieces all roughly the same color. I detest puzzles. But this is a kind of nirvana for David. He murmurs to himself, making soft grunts of approval. He carefully arranges similar pieces into the center of the table. Unlike other puzzle masters, he makes no attempt to outline the work with edge pieces first. He does not consult the picture on the cardboard cover of the puzzle box. I ask him how things are going. He looks up and smiles a twisted leer that might frighten a small child but entirely lacks malice. He rocks back and forth in his seat, holding himself with short wheezing noises that are pure happiness. I look up and notice that the 'paintings' on the dining room walls are actually completed puzzles of intricate design. David, who cannot dress himself, is a puzzle prodigy.

Sherry is a young L'Arche assistant from Cornwall in England. She comes in the front door and joins us at the table. It turns out that Sherry and David are close friends. She tells me about David's history and his remarkable penchant for puzzle art. The conversation turns to his disabilities which result from traumatic brain injury in childhood. David was accidentally dropped on his head as an infant. Sherry acknowledges the tragedy but then tells a story that again reveals the great secret of compassionate love in L'Arche.

> There was a day when I was running around like crazy and all that stuff. Like I told you before, David would stop to make me sit down to give me a gift or give me a blessing or whatever. This was when I was brand new to L'Arche, so I hadn't really experienced it before. He sat me down, and I think that I was pretty emotional and flustered. He

gave me this blessing. I have had so many since then but this was the first, and his favorite song was 'How Great Thou Art'. So he sings this, but it was a medley of 'How Great Thou Art' mixed with his own songs and then he would come back to the final refrain of 'How Great Thou Art'. He sings this song and he was saying, 'Thank you God for this, thank you God for that, thank you God for Sherry, that she's back from the store.' I was floored by the whole thing. I could *feel* God in the room. Then at the end of it, he put the sign of the cross on my forehead. [eyes filled with tears] I was completely stunned because that was something my dad always would do before we went to bed at night growing up. But it was like, how did you know what that would do for me? I am home even though I am not. I belong here. I am home. I am beloved.

Sherry turns her attention to David, tenderly conversing in a muted whisper. Their easy love and familiarity are elements of an unexpected communion. In the economy of the moment they are my teachers. At the puzzle table there are no requirements for vocational achievement. The opinions of others do not matter. Possessions are irrelevant. The communion sacrament is the free gift of compassionate love found in broken fragments miraculously reconstituted through the intuition and generosity of the poor.

4

Saints

*The saints are authors, auctores, increasers of goodness . . . they are impreg-
nators of the world, animators of potentialities of goodness which but for
them would lie forever dormant.*

(William James)[1]

*There are very many who do not refrain from the horrid sacrilege of calling
upon the saints . . . here is where wretched men fall.*

(John Calvin)[2]

I am standing at the lectern on a brilliant spring day in Southern California. The topic is compassionate love. The room is populated with academics, university staff, students, and clergy. Behind me a PowerPoint
presentation flashes images of L'Arche. Halfway through the presentation
a hand shoots up from the audience. It belongs to a middle-aged man
dressed neatly in khakis and pressed shirt. I am not surprised at the
abruptness or urgency of his action. Compassionate love and L'Arche can
be flashpoint topics. Both evoke strong feelings. As a result, I am used to
spontaneous interruptions. The man wonders loudly if I am romanticizing compassionate love in general and its L'Arche manifestation in particular. He is skeptical that these individuals consistently and authentically
love others. I affirm his criticism to the extent that compassionate love
stretches credible notions of human potential, at least if we think about
L'Arche members as modern saints. But this may be problematic. If they
are saints at all, the people of L'Arche are ambivalent saints. Like us, they
are riddled with uncertainty. They tell white lies, hurt others' feelings, and
get speeding tickets. The fallibility of these saints is as psychologically
interesting as their remarkable capacity for compassionate love. Our lofty
notions of love should be tempered by the real struggles of imperfect
people, even the abled and disabled saints of L'Arche.

Regardless of his intentions, the gentleman in the audience made a couple of important observations about compassionate love. At one level we have a tendency to be swept off our feet by love in places such as L'Arche. We extol saints in their capacity for goodness, affirming them as otherworldly celebrities. We use them as benchmarks for sacred and spiritual truths. We measure ourselves against them while in the same breath recognizing our inadequacies. You or I might work valiantly at achieving some fragment of virtue revealed in their lives, only to fail badly and repeatedly. The saints are paragons, archetypes, and heroes beyond the reach of mortals. Examples include Mother Teresa, Martin Luther King, the Dalai Lama, Dame Cicely Saunders, Gandhi, Jean Vanier, and Oskar Schindler. We are keenly aware of their ability to change people and governments. We bestow upon them honor, prizes, and awards for humanitarian greatness. The saints are exemplars – people who show us the meaning of human experience by living well and loving profoundly.

Alternatively, we have an equally powerful tendency to be critical regarding the authenticity of compassionate love and the people who practice it. We are skeptical upon hearing stories of love like those coming from L'Arche. Sainthood is impossibly remote given the reality of human aggression and deception. Historical accounts of saintly individuals are subject to embellishment. We conclude that the public personas of those we deem saintly have been carefully crafted. Observing the political candidate on the campaign trail, we brace ourselves for inevitable revelations of a checkered past to include some combination of drugs, fraud, or sexual misconduct. Compassionate love is particularly susceptible to this kind of thinking. For the scientifically minded, it is tempting to reduce loving behavior to the lowest denominator of understanding, 'demythologizing' its impact through biological origins. Compassionate love is reframed in terms of human evolution and primate behavior. If it exists, compassionate love is best observed through increased blood oxygen in the brain while people play trust games in MRI machines.[3]

Whose compassion? Which love?

Our understanding of compassionate love in L'Arche should be augmented by recognition that nothing about it comes easily. L'Arche is full of interpersonal conflicts, misunderstandings, and problems. Tensions commonly boil over, sometimes with unfortunate outcomes. On the other hand, compassionate love in L'Arche is perplexing and intricate, an unexpected grace resistant to laboratory testing. L'Arche is a community of tremendous mental diversity, eroding the notion that love (or any virtue) is first about lengthy deliberation or reasoning. Between notions of saintly grandeur and firing neurons is the reality of an ambivalent sainthood characterized by personal cost. Throughout the United States, L'Arche caregiver assistants and core members repeatedly informed me that compassionate love is difficult, messy, and often ugly. Compassionate love requires sacrifice. It costs everyone dearly. It is birthed from strife, misjudgement, and weakness.

The unexpected costs of compassionate love were nowhere more evident than in one L'Arche location with a high number of long-term (greater than three years) caregiver assistants. During my stay with this community, a variety of unhealthy behaviors became evident. Several caregiver assistants openly struggled with eating disorders. Some members of the community would spend evenings in a local tavern drinking heavily. I was invited on one of these excursions, told that I should have first-hand experience of how assistants 'compensate' for their work in L'Arche. Community narratives were forged around these tavern trips – a rite of passage for new assistants and an identity for those with long service tenures. In this community, alcohol was a prominent companion to the sustained practice of compassionate love. I have no interest in passing judgement on these caregiver assistants or their behavior. In no way should this single account tarnish the stories of compassionate love recorded in this book. Yet it must be noted that these are ambivalent love practitioners, revealing internal conflict where compassionate goals collide with what one assistant referred to as 'the dark places in my soul'. The personal costs associated with compassionate love were sufficiently real and worrisome that to my L'Arche research project was added the responsibility of designated driver.

This chapter grapples with the problem of saints in our understanding of compassionate love through L'Arche. I contend that our notions of compassionate love should be constantly subjected to the reality of its practice in everyday human affairs. This provides a check against romantic idealization on the one hand, or reduction on the other. The chapter briefly reviews issues in the field of moral psychology that explain the twin risks of idealism or reduction. We will hear from L'Arche caregiver assistants about the details of ambivalent sainthood; what it means to love others when personal costs are high and the community conflicted such that the whole enterprise risks foolishness. I offer interpretation on the meaning of these stories, particularly as they relate to the manner by which love becomes evident. Based on the example of L'Arche, compassionate love is driven by an unexpectedly powerful need for *generativity* expressed in terms of religious calling (see later in this chapter). Even more basic than this, it is about our need to be attached to others. Prior experiences with attachment figures influence the quality of love relationships in L'Arche. Perhaps surprisingly, difficult experiences with love and attachment seem to provide the strongest push for individuals to seek L'Arche and persist through the ups and downs of community conflict.

Real saints

What kinds of saints live in L'Arche? One answer is found through an object lesson from the field of moral psychology. Some readers will recognize the name of Lawrence Kohlberg, the legendary educator and psychologist at Harvard. Nearly two decades after Kohlberg's passing, his theory continues to influence practitioners and scholars around the world. Kohlberg's big idea was that a particular vision of rules and justice (borrowed from the eighteenth-century German philosopher Immanuel Kant and his twentieth-century champion John Rawls) explained the many dimensions of moral behavior, including Browning's notion of compassionate love described in the last chapter.[4] Kohlberg took his idea into the laboratory, studying children to confirm the importance of rules and justice. Believing these to become evident through children's reasoning about moral problems, he developed a series of make-believe dilemmas to outline different levels of moral maturity.

Perhaps the best-known example of these conundrums is the 'Heinz dilemma' where a hapless man must decide whether to steal an expensive cancer drug in order to save his dying spouse. In analysing children's responses, Kohlberg attempted to characterize depth and coherence in moral reasoning. Results from his studies were organized into a six-stage framework for moral development, beginning with simple, concrete explanations and culminating in a dilemma-busting ethic of near superhuman understanding.[5] The development of moral reasoning moved up the stage-like framework with levels of abstraction, meaning that few individuals would achieve moral mountaintops in stages five and six. Kohlberg took this scheme and converted it into an assessment tool known as the Moral Judgement Interview (MJI). On the basis of studies using the MJI, Kohlberg's theory gained widespread support in psychology, eventually influencing education, political science, economics, and public policy.

The inertia of Kohlberg's project was considerable. Emphasis on stage-like development of morality offered practical advantages in moral education. Yet the model was not without problems. One group of critics took aim at the resemblance between Kohlberg's definition of morality and liberal ethics typical of ivory tower locations such as Harvard.[6] This led to cross-cultural studies exploring the relevance of rules and justice reasoning in other countries and with underserved people. Controversy erupted over findings suggesting that communal and religious priorities may be more important than justice in the moral reasoning of Brahmans from India and poor Brazilians.[7] Other concerns emerged with the discovery that individuals with injury to a portion of the brain involved in social behavior were terribly immoral, yet scored in the normal range on the MJI.[8] Kohlberg's preference for a single framework in explaining moral behavior became a lightning rod for debate.

Roughly following the poles of idealism and reduction outlined at the beginning of this chapter, two different reactions to Kohlberg became evident. One approach moved beyond rules and justice reasoning by studying the lives of contemporary saints. The idea was to find out what makes people moral by interviewing individuals widely known for outstanding commitments. Arguably the most famous work in this regard was published more than 15 years ago in *Some Do Care* by Anne Colby and William Damon.[9] The authors spent time with saintly exemplars, some of whom were internationally known for their humanitarian activities in civil rights, work with the poor, and protection of voiceless children in the developing world. Saintly narratives sparkled with stories of care, advocacy, and compassionate love. These were evaluated through a proposal for *moral identity*, or commitment consistent with the self to action that serves the needs of others.[10] The exemplars offered a saintly portrait of moral maturity. But the approach proved vulnerable to the same criticism voiced by the well-dressed gentleman at the beginning of this chapter. The focus on saintly exemplars might tempt psychologists to construct research subjects who do not closely resemble the actual people responding to interviews – individuals who readily admit their mistakes and limitations.

A second approach redoubled efforts to confirm the rules and justice mantra by reducing morality to measures in the brain. These researchers suggested that controversy over a morality of justice was related to limitations of traditional psychological methods, resolved through newer technologies such as brain scanning. A pioneer in the area is Joshua Greene, who took the dilemma concept and adapted it to the study of people lying inside MRI machines. MRI technology can observe changes in soft tissues such as the brain.[11] Greene found that when confronted with awful moral dilemmas, conflict was created in the brain between reasoning and emotion. Hypothetically faced with an out-of-control trolley about to kill five people, subjects were given the choice of doing nothing or pushing a single individual in front of the trolley to stop its progress, thereby saving the five. Morally 'mature' individuals squashed their feelings of empathy for the loss of one individual in favor of the 'reasoned' solution in saving the five. Greene argued that these responses reflect a brain predisposed to a morality of utility reminiscent of nineteenth-century philosopher John Stuart Mill. Not surprisingly, the notion of morality in these studies provoked other criticisms ranging from the extreme dilemmas involved to the possibility that everyday morality is more often about habits operating beneath the surface of awareness.

Any of these approaches (and others not mentioned in this brief overview) could be used as a study framework for compassionate love in L'Arche. We might consider love on the basis of stage-like maturity in Kohlberg. Alternatively, we could consider caregiver assistants as living saints through exemplary love extended to the disabled. Or we could put everyone inside an MRI scanner and observe what parts of the brain are associated with loving behavior. But none of these really makes sense in L'Arche. In this environment, compassionate love is firstly about relationships between core members and caregiver assistants. If we take L'Arche at face value, it is the core members who are the love exemplars. This falls flat in Kohlberg's scheme, given that many (if not most) core members are limited in mental capacities, likely scoring at the lower reaches of the MJI. Moreover, core members are unlikely to qualify for sainthood using the criteria outlined in Colby's and Damon's study. Finally, the many kinds of core member disability in L'Arche make it difficult to identify 'patterns' of love-related brain activity in the unlikely event we could figure out an ethical way to study these vulnerable individuals in the laboratory. Even if we eliminate core members from the picture, it seems clear that L'Arche caregiver assistants are tentative saints riddled with everyday problems and insecurities.

The simple fact is that relatively unremarkable individuals in L'Arche consistently do rather remarkable things. Whether this qualifies core members and caregiver assistants for canonization is open to debate. Rather than idealize or reduce compassionate love in L'Arche, it is probably a better idea to recognize that we all harbor deep and emotionally charged ideas about the nature of compassionate love and do well to check these notions against ordinary people struggling with real challenges. This is not my idea, but one borrowed from Owen Flanagan, a scholar at Duke University interested in moral maturity. Recognizing the basic tendency for researchers to lean heavily into their assumptions for abstract behaviors such as morality, Flanagan argues that theories of morality should be shaped by the experiences of actual people who behave morally in spite of imperfection.[12] His argument is designed to provide a corrective for Kohlberg and other researchers tempted to cling to a pet philosophical theory when studying morality or compassionate love. Researcher preference for Kant or Mill should be tempered by earthy, real-world studies of places like L'Arche.[13] Recognizing our theoretical baggage, the behaviors of real people force us to revise our theories about compassionate love. This requires that we be attentive to the shadow features of love, embracing things like personal cost, conflict, and ambivalence.

What do L'Arche assistants have to say about the darker side of compassionate love? One section of the research interview focuses on life episodes that influence the manner by which individuals come to understand themselves and their love commitments. These interview questions were taken from the work of Dan McAdams, a developmental psychologist at Northwestern University.[14] Of particular interest are two sets of questions dealing with *low point* and *turning point* events. Originally designed to tap what McAdams calls 'narrative identity', I found these questions to outline neatly the ambivalence of L'Arche caregiver assistants, especially those with long service histories. The personal costs of compassionate love are abundantly evident in their responses. The nature of conflict and upheaval in L'Arche is painfully documented with illustrations of love misunderstood or gone bad. At one level, these responses forced me to revisit my own notions of compassionate love taken from Browning and Drigotas. At another level, the assistants offered new insights into the nature of compassionate love related to religious calling and our desire to create close attachments with others.

*   *   *

I'm going to ask you about various events that happened in your life. The event should be an incident that was critical to your development. In each case, the event should have some relation to your beliefs, your commitments, and your desire to care for others. A difficult year in high school, for example, would not qualify as it took place over an extended period of time. Instead, focus on a decision, a conversation, a loss, an accident, or an achievement that had significance. Did this event change you in any way? If so, how? Please be as specific as possible, illustrating why the event is so important.

Low point experience
Tell about a low point in your life story – the worst moment in your life.

*   *   *

Marie is 53 and single. She is a short, plump individual with long service in L'Arche. Her hair is uncolored – streaks of salt are visible against a black-pepper background. She nervously snaps her fingers despite the absence of music. Marie's community doubles as a Catholic retreat center. We are sitting in the chapel next to the main L'Arche residence. The chapel is stark, with a smallish crucifix hanging on the wall beneath a skylight. The room smells faintly of incense. Initially, Marie is slow to open up. She tells me that trust should be carefully cultivated. Fifteen minutes into the interview, however, she becomes more secure – cracking jokes and making light of her own story. Her eyes narrow in response to the above question.

Well, which one of many? I don't know if I'd say it's catastrophic – there are many different things. Like my mother dying was an enormous event and a great sadness. It changed my life, changed what I was to do with my life for years and years. It was a big thing in our whole family, it shook the family. Our family was different after that. I had my mother until I was 21, but my younger siblings bore the brunt of the change. It was a very different experience for them growing up in a single-parent household. I don't think I experienced the same devastation that they did. But it hurt very much. My mother didn't die to spite me or leave me. She hated the idea of leaving her kids. But perhaps this wasn't the lowest of low. I'm thinking now about when I was in a relationship with someone who decided, 'I don't love you that much.' Now *that* was devastating. That was the dark night of the soul. I remember thinking that this is an Easter thing happening to me. A Palm Sunday thing. You're special, you're praised, you're given all kinds of positive attention and love. Then it's fickle, it goes. [long silence] I had the sense of bonding with Jesus in that moment. I don't have those moments all of the time, every time something goes bad. But I'm more inclined to look for Jesus in those suffering moments. Before I came back to this community I was going out with a man who, it turns out, was gay. But he hadn't quite figured that out. He was trying to avoid it because he really wanted to be straight and have a family. It forced me to reconsider L'Arche. In

L'Arche I could give my love to a place where it would be needed and welcomed. Of course I thought to myself, I need to get back into the community. So that was a motivating factor, that out of this place of rejection I still have something, I feel I have something to give. I'm feeling put down in my sexuality and my womanness by your rejecting me. Who needs that? I can go to L'Arche and wow, there's Carrie [core member] and she really needs what I have to give her. It's valued and it's absolutely critical. Without me or someone like me she can't even get out of bed in the morning. In the months after I came here I realized what a relief it was to be in L'Arche. To have an outlet for my love, to have it desired. Outside L'Arche it was just taken for granted.

*　　　*　　　*

Lucinda is 44 with a quick, caustic sense of humor. She is of average height with dyed blonde hair and a prominent silver necklace adorned with a Celtic cross. Lucinda was a corporate lawyer before coming to L'Arche. Her manner reflects this training. She is businesslike and articulate through the interview, moving swiftly between images and event narratives. We are in the dining room of her L'Arche community, a rambling farmhouse surrounded by fields and small stands of tall evergreens. Lucinda once served as director here. The interview question abruptly halts the flow of our conversation. Lucinda sits quietly for a long time before answering. She reaches for a Kleenex as she speaks.

That would've been the last three years of my ten years as [L'Arche community] director. I was buffeted on all sides and not understanding why things were happening as they were. Was it something I did? What could I have done differently? In that struggle I tried my best, but to no avail. I could see our L'Arche community going right down the tubes. If I had walked out I would not have been faithful to the core members in the community. That was the one thing that got me through, my commitment to the core members and the caregiver assistants in the community. If I walked away they would be more persecuted than they were. I shed many tears of anguish during that time. [quietly weeping] Not believing that this is what God wants. He wouldn't want the core members to go somewhere else. It was the low point in my life and I had to trust more than I thought I could trust. I was carried by other people in L'Arche who loved me and loved our core members. That's how I got through. The only place I could pray was on the cross. I thought the community was going to die. We might not exist. It was at a time in my life that I had to say to God, 'This is your work, not mine.' It had come to that point. I still wanted to control everything. That attitude really conflicted with the process by which L'Arche communities are founded. L'Arche happens because of relinquishment, not control. First, someone has to have a vision. Then everyone who comes helps make it grow. It is not just me but everyone. Every member in some way takes this community to the place where it is now. It isn't about me. But in the case of my work as director, I just happened to be the person given the grace to go first.

* * *

Mia is 41, an earth mother with a Southern drawl. Her dreadlocked brown hair extends wildly in many directions. Her eyes are gray and marked with the kind of experience that implies wisdom. Her face is deeply freckled. Mia is wearing a colorful Guatemalan shawl that looks like a serape. She does not wear shoes. She is completing her third year of service in this urban L'Arche community. Mia confesses that she doesn't expect to stay much longer, a comment tinged with reticence. She offers no further details. Mia clearly enjoys her work in L'Arche, although it has not been easy. There is no hesitation when confronted with the low point question.

I don't know if it was hitting bottom with an eating disorder or alcohol. But you want one day? A specific instance? [purses lips in deep thought] One night I was in a bar. I had been at a wedding. I drank all day and went out with a friend from college to a bar after-wards and no matter how much I drank it wasn't working for me any more, and I remember going outside, leaving all my friends and sitting on the steps next to the bar, thinking, 'I have to get a buzz.' I was pissed because it wasn't working for me any more and I was like, 'OK God, there has to be a better way and this sucks if what I have used isn't working any more.' You see, L'Arche is where I began recovery. I think there is such a connection between being broken; L'Arche is about a theology of vulnerability and I think that was one of my most vulnerable moments. I think being in L'Arche led to awareness of my addiction. I have been on a crusade about vulnerability ever since. I began a 12-step program and I have linked the two and that is very much a part of what my spirituality and theology and even ministry is

– that whole wounded healer thing.[15] So I think it relates to my work now in L'Arche and what originally led me to L'Arche.

* * *

Sister Joan is 46 years old, introduced in the last chapter. L'Arche is her life – a truism after nearly 20 years of service. Joan considers L'Arche to be her calling and burden as a person of the cloth. Rain is falling heavily outside as she reflects upon a low point experience that left her clinically depressed.

That would be last fall. You did not ask for a time, but it was definitely the fall. We had a new director who came in August and by October it was clear that it was not a match. She left – actually she was asked to leave – it happened very suddenly in October, and so we didn't have a director. We were in a discernment process [a period of community reflection to decide on calling and direction]. So she was leaving and then two other caregiver assistants who were planning to stay through the summer suddenly changed their minds and told me that they were leaving. It was like everything was falling away. Our founding director came back as interim and he was doing most of the administrative stuff, and life in the homes was very turbulent. It felt like everything was falling apart. It was people leaving, and me feeling like I didn't have a partner. There were lots of people who were committed, on the board, community people who would come in and help. But I wanted to know, who is here for the long haul? Who is my partner? There was a zone council meeting [L'Arche USA region] and our international coordinator was in attendance and he likes to visit communities when he is at meetings. I had tons of support at the highest levels, but nothing at the local level. That was a very low point. It definitely made me question things more. As Jean Vanier says, 'L'Arche is impossible.' So it was like, is this really possible and is it possible for me? Things just got uglier. We had a core person, one of the founding core members, who was in crisis and we were trying to find a new place for him. Everything hit the fan at the same time. Getting on the other side of it and looking back, that is when I was learning to see chaos and change as positive. That is what faithfulness and commitment and love are all about. Even in hard times, to be faithful to what I am called to. I felt called to stay here. Through all that, I still felt called to be here and committed and faithful. So getting through on the other side, I discovered that L'Arche is like that. It is going to happen again, some period of trouble. I think life is like that, but with L'Arche a bit more than most places. Ups and downs. Love prevails.

*   *   *

Timothy is 30 years old, a second-generation Korean American who grew up near Boston. Soft spoken and courteous, Timothy was a literature major in a prestigious public university. He is the youngest of seven siblings, a fact he repeatedly mentions throughout the interview. Timothy states that the decision to live in L'Arche created conflict in his family of origin. Although he offers few details, I can perceive that he does not talk often with his parents. We are sitting in the kitchen of his L'Arche house in the Pacific Northwest. Feeble daylight is rapidly fading. Rain is drumming on the window. He is pensive and deliberate through his response.

I broke up with my girlfriend of six years. It was obviously a very profound relationship to last for six years. It was long distance for the last two years. We were close to getting married, but she suffered from depression and had a hard time. We both realized that she was in no position to follow through on such a commitment. She had to focus on taking care of herself and the relationship was just too much pressure. I will never forget saying goodbye. It was a pretty dark experience. We met in L'Arche. In some ways, it has been hard since I have been back – all the physical remembering. Plus, she was healthy when she was here. It wasn't until later that the depression started manifesting itself. So the memories are bittersweet. But it is also a fact that L'Arche is my family in many ways. Some people really knew what I went through in that relationship. Not a lot, because I didn't talk about it too much. There were a few who walked the journey with us. I lived in Bellingham the year after that and I remember coming back to Yakima as often as I could to see the core members and my friends in the community because I wanted those stable relationships. This is where they were. When I first came to L'Arche it was because of the ideals of Jean Vanier, 'to save the world one heart at a time'. That seemed so profound, and it still does. But more recently I came back to the community for selfish reasons because these are my friends and family. I am at a point in my life where I need to be close to people who care about me. So it was more of an individual reason why I came back. It was actually the people, not the idea behind the people. I wouldn't say that to my parents, because they are family in a way that is profound. I have a big family back home, but it is my immediate family here in L'Arche that I'm close to, not the blood relatives. In L'Arche, whenever we have communion, it is like a little family reunion. I definitely feel like I'm related to the core members and the long-term people. The short-term assistants, it is hard to get close to them. They come and go. It is hard to invest. The long-term assistants, I feel like they are my relations. I bonded, last year, with three new assistants out of the nine. I know there were a few more who got connected to long-term assistants and a few who just didn't. It was actually something we talked about and got concerned about because it is important to have people come in and get connected with people who have been around.

*   *   *

Nicole is 34 years old and divorced. Many in the community refer to her as 'Emeril', honoring her remarkable culinary talents through the famous chef. Core members and assistants will often trade chores so that Nicole can cook. She is tall and athletic with a warm demeanor. Nicole is a long-term assistant with considerable experience in this location. A favorite with the core members, Nicole is tender with Michael, an elderly gentleman who asks to sit with us during the interview. Our conversation is periodically interrupted by comments from Michael. This has the effect of making the interview move in spurts punctuated by verbal affirmation and appreciation of Michael's views.

It was my first year in L'Arche, and I had problems with some of the caregiver assistants I was living with. One of them didn't like me, and he ended up treating me badly and not giving me a chance. I ended up in the house with two people who really didn't like me. I remember feeling trapped in L'Arche. It was so consuming. If you were having a hard time there was nowhere to go. You lived and worked in the same place. I remember when my grandmother died, going to the funeral. It was in Salem so I just drove, but feeling like I had to ask permission to go and feeling trapped. At the funeral they talked about how my grandmother was going to live on through her recipes because she was a great cook, and we all make things that she used to make, and when I got back home to L'Arche that night I found that all my recipes had been thrown in the trash. This was incredibly ironic, right after the funeral. These were things she had handwritten, the last things I had that she had written to me and now they were all in the trash. I didn't have my name on the box and it was in the kitchen in this communal area, but I felt like my life wasn't my own. I wasn't respected, my stuff wasn't respected, I had no privacy, I couldn't get away from any of this, I felt persecuted, I felt misunderstood, I felt like I didn't have any friends, and I felt really far apart from my friends. Certainly my family was always trouble and we were definitely having problems. Before that, I don't think anyone had ever disliked me. I always got along with everyone and I was kind of a people pleaser. You know, I was voted nicest in my class. In college I always got along with my roommates. So it was really devastating to me that I didn't feel accepted by the community and people didn't like me and I remember that night going through the trash and sobbing, getting these recipes out that were stained. [long silence, eyes misting] That was a low point in my life. I almost left. It was really bad. But I also really felt like God had called me and I had taken a long time in making the decision to come. It felt like it was the right thing to do. I ended up going home for a little while, taking a break and coming back. Making the decision to stay, that's when everything went up. Remaining true to myself and remaining true to God. Maybe it has made me a little bit harder. What's on the outside is not as important; getting a person to like me isn't as important. The two people who didn't like me, one of them came back for a visit and took me out to tell me he was sorry for what went on between us, and the other person, we are really close friends now. She is one of my closest friends now, so it all worked out, but it taught me a lot. I had to not care in order for us to be friends in the end. I remember when I said to my director, 'You know the hell that I have gone through with this. I am not leaving before it gets good. I am sure it is going to get good.'

*   *   *

Camille is 54 years old. She is a Latina with long black hair and inquisitive eyes. Camille is lively and curious throughout the interview. It turns out that she studied psychology in college and wanted badly to make a career in the clinical profession. Today, there are no regrets. She considers L'Arche her 'final resting place' after working in retail. Yesterday was her five-year anniversary as a caregiver assistant. An avid sports fan, she is wearing a pullover adorned with her favorite professional football team. We are sitting in the back yard of her L'Arche home in the upper Midwest. The day is cool and slow, perfect for an interview.

I think the one that fits was an experience I had with an assistant in the community. It was an interesting relationship. We had met on a L'Arche retreat a couple of years ago, ended up in the same small group, and we got to know each other pretty intimately through letter writing. Then she ended up moving to another community. She eventually came out here with her fiancé and I was so surprised that they came. I thought, 'Oh my gosh, it is so great that they came out here, they are such great people!' We were sitting at dinner, I was like, 'Why did you guys come?' She turned to me and said, 'It's you, Camille. A large reason why I came was because of my friendship with you.' Wow, that was pretty flattering. Then the bottom fell out a few months later. I happened to move into the same house she was living in. I said, 'I am really glad you are here.' Then she said, 'I know this sounds really blunt, but I just have to tell you. The more I have gotten to know you, the more I realize you are not the kind of person I want in my life and this is not a friendship that I want to have.' Oh God. Being someone who was loved every day of their life, I was like, 'What do you mean? You can't say that!' It was my first experience of major rejection. I didn't understand those words. She put it out there with no warning. Really painful. Yes, I think it turned some things on their head. That might have been the truth, but don't cut me down when I am already on one leg. I have no idea how your life has touched me, but I want to be open to it. That is the great thing about L'Arche. I need to stop spending all my time with people who are like me, raised in the church and really so boring, you know.

*   *   *

Turning point
This is an episode wherein you underwent a significant change in your under-standing of yourself. It is not necessary that you understood the turning point as being significant at the time it occurred. What is important is that now, in retrospect, you see the event as a turning point.

Does this experience relate to your work in L'Arche? If so, how?

*   *   *

92

Steve is 36 years old, of lanky build and curly brown hair. He is from Cape Breton, a ruggedly beautiful region in the Canadian province of Nova Scotia. Steve introduces himself as the 'everyman' of L'Arche. I'm not entirely sure what is meant by this. Our conversation is filled with tangents and rabbit trails. Steve likes to talk and finds it easy to keep things moving. He is completing his twelfth year in L'Arche. He has served in many roles for American and Canadian L'Arche communities, including farm supervisor, caregiver assistant, office temp, and house responsible. Steve thinks hard before responding to my question.

Counseling! When I left L'Arche after five years I traveled and went to France and it was great fun. Then I came back and was with my family. I was trying to make it look like my mother hadn't died. I didn't have work right away, it was an economically tough time for me. When I left L'Arche it felt like I left my church. L'Arche had become my faith community, my religion. It was like, OK, what are you going to do all day long? Left my income and some of my closest friends. I went into depression. Kind of didn't feel like life was worth living, didn't know why I was there. Totally mixed up, totally pained. Feeling like I was walking in a dark place for too long a time. My pride was in the way. I thought, how can I get help? Finally I realized that if this was someone in my L'Arche house, I would connect them with somebody to get help. What are you going to do for yourself? I was hoping that other people would help me. Because I was living at home I thought my father can see how depressed I am, he should help me and call a shrink. He didn't. I realized, OK, it's not going to happen that way. I'm going to have to do it myself. I had my pride, some of the best shrinks in town I already worked with in L'Arche. We'd discuss the core members, and now I thought, 'Oh God, it's me! I can't do this.' Then I remembered this man who had been part of a group for nuclear disarmament. He was always smiling. He was always kind and cheerful to people. I had heard that he was a psychotherapist. I'll call him and run a few things by him and see what he thinks. That was a turning point, because I got insight into how things went in my family, and grief. Grief never comes up alone, always comes up with the L'Arche community. He really helped me to work through a lot of grief. That was a turning point. I think there's a lot of grief in L'Arche, a lot of disappointments, a lot of loss. Core members have them, caregiver assistants have them. We all continue to have them. I think therapy helped me to be more of who I am, more whole.

I approach that from a more whole place. It's been helpful when core members' relatives have died or a core member has died. I feel that I have good, solid experience with these people who are dying. Not a lot of it, I don't think of it every day, but it helps me down the path again. Helps me to be stronger, more aware of how I was conditioned. The patterns I have . . . the habits.

*   *   *

Evie is 27 years old, a relative newcomer to L'Arche with one and a half years of experience. She recently graduated with an associate's degree from a junior college where she studied business and art history. Evie is a recovering alcoholic who grew up in a wealthy suburb of a large American city. She is short, with penetrating green eyes and mousy hair that is prematurely graying. Evie is reserved and soft spoken. At her request, we are in a small office to minimize interruptions from the community. She's initially tentative with her responses. But the turning point question somehow breaks things open.

I think the day, the night I was willing to ask someone to be my sponsor for Alanon [12-step program] was significant because it was the first time I ever had to ask for help. I mean, it seemed so insignificant at the time, but that changed my life. Prior to that I had tried doing 12-step stuff on my own, just me and God, and having to ask another person was a whole other experience of being vulnerable, asking for help and experiencing God in the flesh. Really having a deeper sense of understanding about what it is to be vulnerable and that I am not just the helper but I am the helped. I think it has given me a greater understanding that I have a lot to learn from the core members, that it is more of a mutuality and learning to receive and be vulnerable, and I think that is what L'Arche is all about – allowing other people to be vulnerable. One of my goals is to be more real and more vulnerable, and that is really hard for me, but I want more of that because it is more real and that is what L'Arche teaches.

*   *   *

Diane is 29 years old. She owns the room with her outgoing laugh and razor-sharp wit. We are in the living room of her L'Arche community. I am drowning in an overstuffed sofa that smells faintly of bad perfume. Diane sits straight and narrow on a wingback chair with her legs crossed. Her arms wave emphatically as she talks. Hair is constantly falling into her face and brusquely thrown out of the way. Diane came to L'Arche after working in the Peace Corps. She spent time in Bangladesh and often wears indigenous clothing. A friend to everyone, she pauses her narrative to give hugs, blow kisses, or otherwise interact with passing community members.

> I was already thinking about this. In L'Arche there can be lots of undertones and stuff like that; there's a lot of history, right? Before I arrived in my community, there had been some really hard stuff lived. I think there had been kind of a clique that formed and they were geared up against the director. There was a lot of misunderstanding, a lot of deception. I think there was a lot of hurt, both ways. It was a really hard thing and sometimes you know how things can just fester and stuff. It's something that never should have happened if it had been handled well, or if people had just been up front with what they were feeling. I was coming into L'Arche right after that, and I think a lot of people involved in these troubles had simply left. It was really hard for the director to trust me. It was really hard for me, because I didn't know what was there before, but he thought that maybe some of these people had gotten to me and warned me about him or given some sort of misinformation, which they hadn't. So I was trying to figure this out, why I was being mistrusted and why he was being wary of me. We didn't know each other very well, we didn't know our styles of communicating. Have I done something wrong? It's obvious this person doesn't trust me and thinks I am trying to hide something. I don't know if the situation is making sense, but you know there's all this stuff and he was afraid it was filtering in. There were a couple of meetings we had that were heart-wrenching for me and for him. It was like trying to go in this indirect way about this thing that I didn't really know about but he thought I knew about. Oh, it was just so icky, it was really icky. [squirming in her seat] It was really painful because he had just experienced a hard thing. I understand in hindsight how horrible that must have been for him, and why he would mistrust people because he had been hurt. I had to stick to what was true. I am putting out there what is real for me and this is painful and I am sorry that you don't trust me but it hurts what's happening here. [weeping] Our relationship has grown magnificently since that time. But it was really hard; it was a hard start and it could have ruined any

chance of us becoming friends or having a relationship, it could have. But I think that for both of us, we had to really work on it and I could have completely lost all hope. It was hard for me to stay in L'Arche because when the person who is the head of everything doesn't trust you, it can be really damaging.

I guess the significant thing was that something so difficult has grown. We trust each other now. I feel that. For him to be able to understand that I need that to be able to feel secure. Also, I think I have grown in my own ability to be authentic and put things out there and name them directly and not try to expect people to be able to figure things out. No more speaking around things; really be true to what you are feeling and speak from your heart. I have had many experiences since then of having to address something or challenge someone or whatever and I think that has helped me to be able to do that well, because I hate it. Also to understand being on the other side of that, and how you really need to be honest and direct but sensitive and take the best interpretation of people. Yes, putting stuff out there and being authentic is really the way to go and it is hard; I am still not very good at it, but I am getting better. It will never be easy.

*   *   *

Jeannie is 28 years old. She is of medium height with bobbed hair. Jeannie wears glasses and looks studiously serious until she smiles. She is a self-proclaimed 'bookworm who enjoys a good laugh'. We are on the porch of a massive, slightly dilapidated Craftsman house with many rooms and much noise in the heart of a large American city. We have commandeered rocking chairs for the interview. She rocks rapidly back and forth, twirling her hair as she speaks. Jeannie is very interested in the study, for reasons that become clearer in her response to the interview question.

I would say my life changed significantly, I think, my first year out of college. I learned a lot about what I wanted to do in my life. My parents' expectations and what I was going to do with my life was put before me. I didn't know what I was doing, so I had until that point been going with the flow and then all of the sudden, BOOM, here I am totally on my own and I can do anything I want and it was totally overwhelming to me. I am very indecisive anyway – it is hard for me to pick out a tube of toothpaste at the store without going through all the choices. [long chuckle] My parents had all these expectations that I would be successful and take the academic route and get a PhD. In college I was doing research with infants for a famous child psychologist, a developmental psychologist. But at the same time I also had this side of me . . . I was a Christian and wanted to take that seriously and also wanted to serve other people and I was working at this group home with schizophrenics. So it was weird. I went from this totally academic job where I dressed up and had all this knowledge and people came to me and I did research on their infants. They wanted to know if their baby is smart, if their baby is normal, and I was the expert and I was a supervisor with people who worked under me. Then I worked in this schizophrenic group home where it was very low pay and you weren't shown a lot of respect for what you did and I had no power. I was an employee. It gave me a lot of self-worth to feel like I was smart, to feel like I was successful, and I had approval from people, people thought it was interesting what I was doing. Of course, my parents were proud of me. I went to this academic conference in New Mexico called SRCD, the Society for Research in Child Development. It was really eye-opening. I worked for this professor a lot of people knew and so my name tag had her name tag underneath, so people would stop me because of her. There was a lot of name dropping and I was totally out of the loop. I didn't know who any of these people were and they would refer to these great psychologists by their first names, and I started to see how people weren't out for any truth there. In my lab they did these experiments for years and years and we had a budget of $2 million to do these projects that took forever to complete. I went back last year and they are doing exactly the same thing! They weren't doing really important things. Maybe some of it might have practical application, but I don't know, there were a lot of people trying to prove other people wrong and doing the same study with small differences to try to show that other people had done the study wrong. They weren't trying to figure out something that would be important for babies. You know, who cares if babies learn 'object permanence' [awareness of an object when no longer in view] at three months or if they are born with it? I felt really disenchanted with academics. I thought this was pointless. I remember talking to my boss and she said, 'You know, Jeannie, there are two kinds of people. There are some people who are happy contributing to the body of knowledge. And there are some people who like to serve. Who like to help people. I kind of think you are in that second group of people.' I guess at that point I had already decided to go to L'Arche.

The SRCD conference was a deciding moment and then I made lots of choices that took me away from academics. I probably never will go back and get a PhD. I do think I will go back to school, but I don't think I am going to be doing research and getting a doctorate. I've turned away from my parents. I mean they were really disappointed in the choice I made in coming to L'Arche – no money or worldly success or approval. I am probably going to be pretty poor most of my life and I am marrying a minister and I am never going to have my name in a journal, but I think it was a really good choice.

*   *   *

The narratives left me with little alternative but to take a strong dose of my own medicine. Flanagan's dictum regarding the struggles and experiences of real people struck home after listening to the assistants. Their responses were a warning against romanticizing or mistrusting compassionate love. I do not believe that the stories in this chapter should cause us to throw out theoretical baby and bathwater, but the reflections of wounded and formerly addicted caregiver assistants are worthy of careful consideration. At particular risk is my preference for Browning's notion of compassionate love as mutual interest in the other. It seems clear that L'Arche assistants rely on a variety of means to persevere through awful upheavals in the community. In the worst of these storms, L'Arche may be an arid place for compassionate love. Sister Joan, Diane, and Nicole mention periods of history where L'Arche communities are barely functioning. The love offered by assistants in these circumstances is potentially misunderstood, ignored, or even rebuffed. We do not sense much in the way of mutuality or interest. There is no 'tit-for-tat' exchange that provides assistants with reward for their willingness to extend themselves on behalf of others. With the advantage of hindsight, assistants seem to acknowledge elements of growth resulting from the tumult. But at that moment the outlook was dim at best.

What factors encouraged assistants to stick things out? Sister Joan, Nicole, and others speak of a *calling* or sense of renewed purpose to stay with L'Arche despite the difficulties. This emphasis on calling was much stronger than I expected. Granted, L'Arche is a religious community and 'calling' is a well-known concept in Christian theology. In Protestantism, calling refers to the believer's understanding of divine guidance or direction, often related to vocational commitments. In Catholicism, the term is usually confined to the work of clergy or other ecclesial obligations. In either case, calling is *ideological*, or given to the idea of God's eternal purposes in human affairs. What surprised me was that assistants commonly offered the notion of calling in response to a question I never asked – namely, why on earth would they stay in L'Arche and offer compassionate love when the environment was (at least for a time) downright hostile?

The notion of calling is more than a religious benchmark for obedience. It is an aspect of what Dan McAdams refers to as *generativity* (mentioned earlier in the chapter). We do things because we want to generate something new, make a contribution, leave a mark, or bring joy to difficult circumstances. In hundreds of interviews with people asked to talk about their sense of personal identity, McAdams found that generativity was a central factor in developing maturity. Generativity tended to become more pronounced with age as people sought to leave a legacy for others. Generative individuals had clearly defined goals and interpersonal objectives. Generativity coincided with a mature sense of purpose. Nicole's parting comments offer evidence of a religious calling that is generative: 'I am not leaving before it gets good. I am sure it is going to get good.' Her decision is not entirely rational. Mutual love interests are not abundant in her community. There are scarce opportunities for perceptual or behavioral affirmation. Yet she knows that something larger is at stake. Her conviction bridges deep religious commitment (evidenced in other aspects of her narrative and person) with a stubborn conviction that L'Arche is a place of generative potential. L'Arche is worth waiting for, even when cherished recipes from her grandmother are thrown out like common trash. It is probably no coincidence that the L'Arche assistants who show the greatest sense of calling and generativity are those who have served for many years. Generativity and maturity are developmental companions across the life span.

These assistant 'saints' offered other amendments to my understanding of compassionate love. It is clear that L'Arche functions as a surrogate family for some assistants; a place where love is desired. L'Arche is a point of reckoning for assistants who are beginning the long road to recovery from addiction. Assistants come to L'Arche for a variety of reasons, not all of which can be characterized as altruistic. The narratives in this chapter suggest that personal needs compel many to serve. These needs are related to interpersonal deficits, past traumas, or failed relationships. A common basis for relational needs is offered in Diane's willing admission that she craves security. This is a clue that L'Arche is a nexus for resolution of *attachment* issues in the experience and practice of compassionate love.

The need to be securely attached to others is well known in psychology. For decades researchers noted the importance of bonding between parents and offspring for a range of primate species, humans included. In the 1960s, a British psychiatrist named John Bowlby founded a group of Oxford thinkers charged with developing a better understanding of human attachments. The group was diverse, ranging from philosophers to zoologists. The outcome became known as *attachment theory*, a behavioral system evolved to regulate our responses to environmental threats or stress. People differ in their response to threats based on attachment styles reflecting experiences with past attachment figures, both romantic and parental. After several decades of research, two dimensions most consistently reflect an individual's overall attachment style. Individuals with high relationship *anxiety* have histories involving ambivalent or inconsistent care. Persons with high relationship *avoidance* harbor distrust, anticipating rejection from others. These dimensions have many shades and textures, making it difficult to categorize attachment styles in a meaningful way. But the research literature does suggest that while the majority of the population demonstrates secure attachment (low to moderate anxiety and avoidance), a substantial minority are 'insecure' in their attachment styles, with some combination of elevated anxiety, avoidance, or both.

Unexpectedly, a considerable number of long-term caregiver assistants seem to have insecure attachment styles, for which L'Arche becomes a kind of compensation strategy. This is unexpected because the psychological literature suggests that it is the securely attached individuals who are most empathic or likely to volunteer.[16] Many of the assistants report problems with family, other assistants, and romantic figures that contain hints of anxiety or avoidance. It may be that L'Arche is a safe haven to work out deeper relational deficits that assistants bring with them. Despite internal struggles in L'Arche, the prospect of relational healing and redemption is even weightier, potentially offering a hope worthy of perseverance. True to Flanagan's point, the real-world context of L'Arche supplies evidence that potentially overturns conventional wisdom regarding compassionate love. It would be a mistake to name this love as romanticized altruism. It is equally problematic to reduce compassionate love by trying to divorce it from the relational landscape of L'Arche. Effort to label love on the basis of behavior-specific gene sequences or neurological structures misses the unique, adaptive requirements of these communities.

The saints sing karaoke

I am with the ambivalent L'Arche assistants briefly mentioned at the beginning of the chapter. We are traveling to a local watering hole, a peeling obelisk in an industrial backwater. The burnt-orange building is shaped like a giant beer stein. This is apparently intentional, a bad idea nurtured during a fashion era marked by tailfins on family sedans. A wretched neon sign flickers dismally in the mist. The car is buzzing with conversation. We enter the stein and sit at a table close to a stack of amplifiers stuck on REO Speedwagon and Supertramp. The place reeks of cheap American beer. A long-haired individual dressed in black is setting up a karaoke machine on a small platform. I am told that several L'Arche assistants are expert karaoke singers with favored playlists maintained by the tavern DJ. One of their number jumps onto the platform and begins to sing. He is surprisingly good, closely following Sting's quirky vocals while covering old hits from The Police. The small crowd roars approval. Alcohol is flowing freely.

Our group is seated at a booth in the stein. The fake leather upholstery is cracking and peeling. Jalapeño peppers and nachos litter the table. The assistants gradually disperse, taking turns at karaoke, dancing, or mingling with other groups. I am left at the table with one caregiver assistant who seems a bit more subdued. Our conversation proceeds at elevated decibels to match the din of the amplifiers. It is tavern talk – a discussion of sports, weather, and food preferences in that order. The assistant pauses and gives me a long look. Without warning, she volunteers insight into her own ambivalence and process of growth in L'Arche.

I'm sure you're wondering why we're here. [gestures to indicate the tavern] I've wondered that myself. I think I've figured it out, why this is an important part of my work. I'm learning to be gentle with myself. I come from a family that had huge expectations for me, they wanted me to be a doctor or lawyer or some kind of mega-manager with a multinational company. My family wasn't very gentle with each other or with me. But in L'Arche I've learned that these things aren't what it means to be human. I've learned that I'm very human; I tend to hurt people and can be pretty emotionally fragile. What's more, I've learned that others in L'Arche are the same way. Instead of making myself into some kind of superhero with a blue cape and red tights, I'm learning to be gentle with myself. To recognize that I'm like this and that others are too. Not be judgemental. Being gentle means learning how to love others just as they are. Most important, it means doing the same with myself.

Her closing diatribe is overpowered by the karaoke music coming from the amplifiers. For some minutes I cannot respond. Her honesty is as striking as her ambivalence. I resonate with her conclusions, particularly the need to be gentle with oneself. The assistant's insight punctures my notions of compassionate love, reminding me that authentic care is closely aligned with human suffering and weakness.

5

Out of Ashes

There are two kinds of people in L'Arche. The larger category includes people who have experienced very significant pain in their lives. I came and discovered that pain was everywhere.

(Emily, a 25-year-old L'Arche assistant)

Job took a potsherd with which to scrape himself, and sat among the ashes.
(Book of Job)[1]

The dog is barking. He competes with the receding echo of the doorbell. Unlike many American L'Arche communities, this home keeps pets. The front door opens with a burst of activity. The caregiver assistant is a middle-aged woman who attempts to offer greeting, manage the door, and keep the dog from taking an unsupervised tour of the neighborhood. Once we are inside, the barking fades. The assistant is named Tina. She explains that the dog (known as Amigo) was rescued by the community as a stray. Today he is handsome with mottled coat and laughing eyes. At the time of his rescue, the dog was near death. The ensuing recovery took months and required heroic interventions. Amigo's recuperation happened in step with the awakening of Stacy, a core member mired in depression. The dog became a fixture in Stacy's life, pulling her from the depths into a world of sustained interest and novelty. Together, dog and woman were restored to health. During the telling of this story Amigo watches me closely, as though searching my face for indication of understanding and agreement.

Tina leads me through the house to a sunroom converted into an office. The sunroom edges the back yard, an inviting place harboring enormous oak trees and an overgrown bower. I scan the walls while she makes coffee. Pictures are everywhere. These are spontaneous family portraits of the community at picnics, birthday parties, and summer vacations. The smiles are unforced, the relationships authentic. The frames tell stories celebrating people over achievement – an unmistakable signature of compassionate love. Tina and I chat about the pictures. At some point our conversation crosses a thin line from casual exchange to the formality of a research interview. She makes ongoing reference to the photos surrounding us.

I was raped in high school. Even though my family moved around a lot and there was suffering and isolation, as a people person I was able to fit in and make friends quickly, even if I was dying inside. After the rape I gained 30 pounds. I probably became severely depressed, severely dissociated. This was an insane time. I never told anybody. My junior and senior year of high school I didn't have a single friend. There were some people I socialized with a little bit at school. I went from being someone who dated to someone who was overweight, invisible, severely depressed, and nobody noticed. If I let myself re-enter it, the pain was huge. What it gave me was that I experienced what it was like to be entirely on the outside looking in. Things looked really different that way. I think it brought me to a whole different level. It's interesting, I had a lot of feeling for people who were on the outside; I was the kid who couldn't stand people being picked on. But I hadn't been completely that way. I just felt ugly and awful and icky. It was humiliating. I can still remember not having a date for my prom. Or not going to a single dance. I think it gave me a whole experience of being a part of a world.

I look at the L'Arche core members, I mean, what more rejected group is there? What group wears their pain in such a manner? Not that anybody should be ashamed, but let's face it, most people who are handicapped feel shame. And they wear it. To feel voiceless, to feel invisible, to feel unattractive. I used to think, I'll never get married. No man could ever love me. I've dwelt in the shadow lands. But I think it impacted receptivity in my heart. Much of that wasn't at a conscious level or awakening my own experience. That came later, over the years. I've been much more freed up at L'Arche. It's impacted my ability to be more forgiving. I think the community allows people to be free. It's a movement into more freedom, more joy. More peace, more tolerance for other people. I get less worried about things now. I've always said God will provide, but now I'm living in it more.

Despite her tears, Tina's gestures are broad and expansive. She unconsciously motions toward the family pictures on the wall. Our conversation is framed by a cohort of disabled core members who know the contours of rejection and suffering, but also the possibility of worth and wholeness. Her time in L'Arche is about healing from shame.

Tina's narrative is a story of suffering, growth, and recovery. These elements are bounded by her experience of compassionate love in community. The primary catalyst in Tina's restoration is the disabled core members of L'Arche. Core members blaze a trail from shame to a fuller, richer existence. This doesn't come easily. Core members have walked the same ground of abuse. They know the humiliation of public leers and whispered judgements. They understand the pain of strangers who refuse to make eye contact. They might look for ways to remain hidden, run away, or play dead. Through her encounter with core members, Tina participates in community where compassionate love is practiced with the deepest respect for others. She makes an important discovery regarding the nature of shame. Negative habits can be identified and rewritten. Feelings of personal loathing will yield to acts of compassion. Unequivocal love is capable of healing the most disordered self-perceptions.

In L'Arche, the wisdom of disability is that shame can be changed into a moral maturity of compassionate love. My objective for this chapter is to consider Tina's narrative on the basis of three guideposts. These include habits informed by *moral intuition*, feelings in *moral emotions*, and identity through *moral self*. Each of these guideposts is considered in separate sections. The sections are introduced with references to Tina's story, followed by discussion leading to specific observations from L'Arche.[2] Unlike other chapters in this book, my focus is given to a single assistant narrative. Tina's story serves as a representative case study for a majority of L'Arche assistants and core members – people with deep and extensive wounds often characterized by shame.[3] Because L'Arche is the context for this discussion of shame and moral maturity, I will assume that much of Tina's process is unique to these communities. In L'Arche, goal-corrected partnerships emphasizing compassion and love influence transition from shame to maturity. Core members are the main example and inspiration for how this might work.

The L'Arche paradox

Dozens of caregiver assistants insist that disabled core members are the prophets and teachers of L'Arche. Core members provide instruction on living well with disability. This unexpected characterization anticipates movement from shame to moral maturity. Core members know suffering in profundity. A considerable number have histories of abuse. Nearly all understand what it means to be different from everyone else. This is more than an occasional feeling of being odd or unusual. Disability might be evident in physical, psychological, or mental difference. Some core members are afflicted by a combination of all three. Unable to conceal their disabilities in public, core members at best evoke sympathy, at worst outright fear. Many of their experiences are etched with the measured indifference of others. The quiet message is devastatingly simple. You are not productive. You are not intelligent. You do not belong.

Once in L'Arche, core members undergo their own process of growth and maturation in the presence of compassionate love. For some the transition comes easily. But for individuals such as Stacy, extended time may be required to rehabilitate the kind of trust necessary to function within community. Caregiver assistants regard core members as leaders on a long journey, traversing the distance between shame and wholeness. Examples abound. There is Gracie, abandoned by her parents and institutionalized for the majority of her life. Mute and aggressively antisocial at the time of her arrival in L'Arche, Gracie is now the neighborhood chatterbox. Her hospitality is legend. There is Danny, first introduced in Chapter 2. His background is imperfectly known in bits and pieces. Danny carries scars from cigar burns and months confined in a neighbor's dimly lit basement. Today he is a curious and gentle soul. These and many other core members remind their communities of real potential for healing. They flourish in their understanding and practice of compassionate love.

In the previous chapter I suggested that core members are at the center of a paradox. These individuals are not regarded for their ability to reason through moral dilemmas weighing justice or consequences.[4] They are not under consideration for the Nobel peace prize or awards of humanitarian excellence.[5] Yet core members challenge their communities to practice compassionate love in recklessly abundant ways. These people live at the hub of a movement which resides on the extreme fringe of positive human potential. Core members inspire others to embrace suffering and weakness toward a life of character and meaning. They show liberation from shame. The shockwave from core member example carries sufficient energy that highly educated caregivers will spend five, ten, fifteen, and even twenty years living in L'Arche without benefits or measurable income. Paradoxically, those deemed by society as unfortunate and malformed often exhibit healing toward a moral maturity of uncommon virtue.

The L'Arche paradox turns compassionate love upside down. The disabled set a standard of compassion and love which stretches the limits of conventional understanding. Yet this may be problematic. The paradox is almost entirely reliant upon the credibility of caregiver assistants. Is reference to core members as prophets a sentimental projection from these well-meaning individuals? There are two possible answers. Either assistants like Tina are overstating the influence of core members, or our notions of moral maturity generally exclude the example and potential of disabled humanity. Let us consider the first possibility, that assistants exaggerate the positive impact of core members. Psychologists are familiar with the terrain of distortion and hyperbole. People under psychological study are widely known to put their best foot forward. Sensing what the researcher is after, individuals will try to match personal attitudes with apparently favored project outcomes. The scientific guild refers to the phenomenon as *social desirability bias*. It is a lightning rod for controversy. Some hard-nosed scientists dismiss major sociological and psychological studies because of the problem. Others use the issue to justify intentional deception in research.

Social desirability bias unquestionably influenced the research presented in this book. Although I made little of it, L'Arche members likely understood my reasons for visiting their communities. This is because L'Arche is renowned for things like *compassion* and *love*. Despite the fact that my interview avoided these terms, assistants probably knew they were on the table or, at the very least, somewhere in the room. The possibility of social desirability bias should temper discussion regarding the L'Arche research project. But while this is an important admission, it does not resolve the argument that Tina is overstating the role of core members in her recovery. Social desirability bias is directed toward easily perceived researcher intentions.[6] It is highly unlikely that Tina or any other L'Arche caregiver would expect an outsider to understand the radical idea that core members are guides in recovery from shame. It is even more remote that the research study would recognize this notion as an expected outcome. As it happened, the prominence of core members in the moral development of L'Arche caregivers was slowly revealed over months of interviews.

The second answer is more plausible. In this view, science minimizes or excludes the moral potential of disabled core members. To be fair, it is unlikely that such exclusion is associated with prejudice against the disabled. Scientists interested in moral issues are, for the most part, decent individuals with sincere concern for others. More likely, it reflects limited notions of moral maturity in social research. L'Arche is a strange duck. These communities speak a unique language of compassionate love. This language comes from a particular moral and religious vision in Roman Catholicism. Many of the narratives recorded in this book allude to religious images and spiritual struggles. Moral maturity in L'Arche is framed by historical figures like Thomas Aquinas and Aristotle.[7] These are champions of virtue and character. The moral language of L'Arche, and the practices which inform it, are some miles away from the scientific mainstream. Contemporary scientific research understands morality through democratic principles of justice or consequences of human action. These differences make it unlikely that science will easily recognize what is moral about L'Arche and its disabled core members.[8]

There is an important caveat to this discussion. Morality is highly abstract, at least if one's yardstick measures things like justice or the consequences of behavior. But abstractions aren't worth much in L'Arche. The communities are mentally diverse. The broad range of mental differences in L'Arche shifts priorities away from moral domains or consequences toward concrete action and experience. Core members offer moral instruction through their behavior. But they typically do not offer explanations for what they do. Most days, they cannot tell us why they extend compassion, love, or forgiveness. They recognize their limitations and disabilities while choosing to move beyond shame. They embrace a simple hope of growth and healing. Taking full advantage of their abilities, the core members of L'Arche look for concrete ways to make a positive and lasting mark on the community. This means that community members who journey from shame to moral maturity are watching each other for examples of how to live well. Instead of books they read faces.[9] Rather than reflect on consequences, they are motivated by feelings. Healing and maturity grow when individuals feel good about themselves through respectful treatment of others.[10]

The L'Arche paradox directs our attention to the moral example of disabled core members. This moves consideration of shame and maturity out of conventional scientific boxes. Gracie and Danny are mostly oblivious to broader implications of harm, rights, or justice.[11] They don't lose sleep ruminating over the moral consequences of their actions.[12] Instead, Gracie tenderly holds the hand of a weeping community member. Danny wordlessly moves into the kitchen and pours a fresh cup of coffee for an individual who angrily spilled hers at the dinner table. These core members model behavior which retrieves compassion, love, and forgiveness from the depths of shame. A lot of this happens without reflection or deliberation. Although Tina lacks mental disability, her journey of recovery shares much with the core members of L'Arche. This process can be described with guideposts relevant to both core members and care-giver assistants. These include habits in *moral intuition*, feelings in *moral emotions*, and identity in *moral self*.

A matter of habit

Tina makes a profound admission toward the end of her story. She tells us that the process of growth from shame to moral maturity happened beneath her conscious awareness.

> I used to think, I'll never get married. No man could ever love me. I've dwelt in the shadow lands. But I think it impacted receptivity in my heart. Much of that wasn't at a conscious level or awakening my own experience. That came later, over the years. I've been much more freed up at L'Arche. It's impacted my ability to be more forgiving.

The account describes excruciating shame. For a time Tina lives in darkness, openly questioning her worth to others. Then healing begins. The transition is subtle, lacking a defined turning point. There is no mention of insight in therapy. The story is devoid of miracles or spiritual revelation. Her narrative is without reference to prolonged illness or near-death experience. Nevertheless, change is afoot. She is increasingly recep-tive to others, following the example of core members. Forgiveness becomes a valid option in relationships. Why isn't she aware of these enor-mously significant changes until years later?

One answer is found in the idea that moral maturity happens on the basis of learned habits regulated by *intuitions*.[13] Very simply, moral intu-itions are sensations at the edge of consciousness. These sensations help people evaluate social situations and the behaviors of others. Intuitions are forged through sensations of disgust. An ability to 'do the right thing' is guided by intuitive sense of whether the behavior is disgusting or appeal-ing. Tina offers an illustration. Waiting for the ATM machine, she wit-nesses a situation with moral implications. The man standing at the ATM is elderly and feeble. After taking his money, he accidentally leaves his card in the slot and shuffles away. The ATM beeps request for further instructions. The man is evidently deaf. It would be a simple thing for Tina to withdraw additional money from the old man's account. No one is watching. Without hesitation, she closes the account and grabs the card. She follows after the man and returns the card to him. She does not pause for navel gazing. Tina quickly responds to the situation with a sequence of moral actions. She operates on habit informed by a catalogue of intuitive sensations lodged in memory.

Moral intuition deflates the common assumption that good behavior is always preceded by a long think. In workaday circumstances, moral action happens mostly under the surface of conscious awareness. Core members like Gracie and Danny can't talk much about their compassionate and loving behaviors save to acknowledge that actions were 'right'. But this isn't necessarily because of mental limitation. When asked why she helped the elderly gentleman, Tina is similarly tongue-tied. Habits directed by intuition do not require great intelligence, yet they are profound beyond words. The implications of moral intuition are every-where. A boy spots a classmate threatened by bullies on the football field. Without further thought, he sprints to intervene. A trial lawyer perceives weakness in the character of a star witness. Defending a vulnerable client, she spontaneously redirects her cross-examination, successfully exposing inconsistencies in the testimony. Behavior happens because of fleeting sensations of rightness rather than extensive thought and reflection. The intuition argument is rooted in human evolution.[14] For our distant ances-tors, morality required swift adaptation to changing social circumstances. The luxury of deliberation is too slow when potentially unfriendly strangers are pounding at the door. Explanations and reasons offered for moral behavior happen after the fact; a backward-looking justification for rapid decisions made through habits guided by moral intuition.

The moral intuition proposal is currently stirring the scientific pot – an intriguing alternative to justice or consequences. The proposal adds some-thing to our understanding of compassionate love in L'Arche. In line with the L'Arche paradox, intuition accommodates the mental diversity of these communities. That is, intuition offers a basic explanation for why persons with mental limitations are able to love well and compassionately. For that matter, intuition does the same for persons without mental limi-tations. Tina's response to the elderly gentleman at the ATM is clearly the right response. It is the loving response. Did it require highly abstract cal-culations and deliberations? No. Does it necessitate advanced degrees? Absolutely not. Compassionate love in L'Arche is rooted in habits which are intuitive in nature. We do not know for sure if Gracie or Danny would react to the ATM situation in the same way as Tina. But it seems reason-able that these core members, when confronted by the elderly gentleman, would behave similarly. Certainly Gracie and Danny practice habits of compassionate love in their community. These habits are not very different from the loving habits practiced by Tina. It is habit, rather than brilliant solutions to moral dilemmas or anticipated consequences, that makes compassionate love a growing possibility for core member and assistant alike.

Moral intuition shines brightly in movement from shame into a life of compassionate love. Tina's maturation process is, for many months and years, mostly unconscious. Slowly changing habits gradually open the doors to fuller engagement with others. Tina's conscious knowledge of the change is underlined through her mention of *receptivity*. Based on the context of her remarks, receptivity is awareness that others (core members) have also experienced the agony of shame. This awareness makes forgiveness possible, leading to freedom. Tina's development implies acquisition of new habits directed by intuition. Many of these habits are modeled through core member example or opportunities presented through disability. The practice of compassion and love makes it easier to understand that others struggle with personal shame. Over months and years, Tina becomes receptive to her own worth and the value of others around her. She is able to receive the core members on their terms, much as she was unequivocally received by the community in the aftermath of her shame experience.

But this is not the punchline. Moral intuition probably oversimplifies the depth and breadth of Tina's recovery process, with disgust a prime culprit.[15] Certainly disgust may influence the acquisition of loving habits. But it seems unlikely that this sensation acts alone or without self-interest. Tina's growing ability to be more receptive to the suffering of others involves many different sensations and feelings. These impact her opinion of self. Compassionate love is more than an intuitive habit which attempts to avoid disgusting alternatives. Tina does not assist core members at the dinner table simply to keep them from drooling. More likely, disgust anticipates other sensations and feelings. Receptivity happens because Tina takes pride in the growth and recovery of core members in her community. Receptivity occurs when Tina's intuitive habits of love are aligned with her personal goals and identity. Maturity flourishes when Tina goes to bed knowing that she loved others well.

*   *   *

The interview is completed. Tina moves into the kitchen, offering to help with lunch. Free until mid-afternoon, I follow her lead. My assignment is to assist a core member named Annabelle. Although details are sketchy,

Annabelle struggles greatly with hand–eye coordination. Mealtimes are particularly difficult. Much effort is directed toward helping Annabelle become independent at the table. Her place setting features a special fork and knife with dulled points and edges to avoid injury. Her plate is made of plastic. Adorned with Winnie the Pooh and several capricious bees, the plate is divided into sections. The sections make it easier to manage food items. Several napkins are stacked to the right of the plate. Annabelle's chair is positioned over a tarpaulin to make clean-up easier. Her cup is a gaudy travel mug with tightly fastened lid – insurance against a knock-down. While I am getting everything ready, Annabelle joins me at the table. Taking her seat, she wordlessly motions toward an oversized bib hanging on the wall. I take the bib and carefully secure it around her neck. During this process, I notice beautifully stenciled letters on the front of the bib. The letters are hand-sewn in shiny purple satin. They spell, 'Celebrate!'

We are a skeleton crew at lunch. Several core members are off at work in a local floral shop. Two assistants are in the town running errands. The rest of us are seated with paper plates and picnic cutlery. Lunch is a simple affair – leftover spaghetti from two nights past. Tina sits directly across from me. To my right is Annabelle. Her struggle to manage basic mealtime movements is considerable. It takes nearly a minute for her to grasp the fork with painfully slow adjustments. Her patience is inspiring. It is evident that Annabelle enjoys the mealtime experience of community and feels empowered by her companions. Serving bowls of food are beginning to make rounds in the usual family-style format. A large platter of spaghetti reaches me. I offer to put some on Annabelle's plate, mindful that I must balance courtesy with community efforts to enhance her mealtime independence. Fortunately I have not overstepped any boundaries. She grins widely and gives thanks.

The meal begins. Annabelle is trying something new. She attempts to twirl the spaghetti on her fork, using a spoon to keep it from falling off. Tina is watching closely, a smile tugging at the corner of her mouth. Five minutes pass without success. Annabelle redoubles her efforts, concentrating intensely on fork, spoon, and pasta. She is visibly frustrated. Tina swiftly moves her chair around the table to Annabelle's side. With the fewest possible interventions Tina helps keep the fork on target with the spoon. Respecting Annabelle's plainly obvious wish to summit this mountain on her own, Tina sits back with apprehension. The fork wobbles as it travels to Annabelle's mouth. Victory! She eats and then slowly repeats the entire process, this time without intervention. The table bursts into applause. Tina comes out of her seat with excitement, hugging and kissing Annabelle. The clapping continues, growing into an ovation worthy of Bach at the San Francisco Symphony. The two faces to my right are nearly superimposed. Annabelle and Tina are laughing in unison. Their eyes glitter with pride.

*　　*　　*

Shame, guilt, and pride

Shame is powerful and debilitating. With startling clarity, Tina shows how this single emotion is able to steamroll the life of an American teen.

> My junior and senior year of high school I didn't have a single friend. There were some people I socialized with a little bit at school. I went from being someone who dated to someone who was overweight, invisible, severely depressed, and nobody noticed. If I let myself re-enter it, the pain was huge. What it gave me was that I experienced what it was like to be entirely on the outside looking in. Things looked really different that way. I think it brought me to a whole different level. It's interesting, I had a lot of feeling for people who were on the outside; I was the kid who couldn't stand people being picked on. But I hadn't been completely that way. I just felt ugly and awful and icky. It was humiliating. I can still remember not having a date for my prom. Or not going to a single dance. I think it gave me a whole experience of being a part of a world.

Her account is a cold bath. Shame profoundly shapes Tina's adolescent experience. What other feelings are involved in her movement from shame into moral maturity characterized by compassionate love?

Psychology is acquainted with a class of feelings known as *moral emotions*. Researchers interested in children and youth are particularly concerned with these feelings, owing to their powerful influence over the life course. Shame, guilt, and pride are the best-known denizens of the moral emotion category.[16] These debut in childhood and mature through adolescence into adult experience.[17] Each of these emotions is immediately recognizable. *Shame* is a paralyzing sense of defectiveness in the self. Shamed individuals feel exposed. They are humiliated. Their sense of unworthiness is amplified by external influences which reject, disapprove, and cheapen. Tina shares a gut-wrenching description of shame which relegates her to the social margins. Previously an outgoing individual, she is crushed. The harrowing aftermath of rape involves a starkly redefined sense of self. Words like 'ugly', 'awful', and 'icky' describe the extent of the damage. Tina is alienated from others. She is locked out of her own high school experience, watching prom dances and peer relationships from across a gulf of inner emptiness.

Guilt differs from shame. In contrast to the self-hatred of shame, guilt focuses on actions and behaviors apart from the self. The guilty are remorseful for what they do. Guilt is behind the child's fleeting withdrawal from the cookie jar when a parent enters the kitchen before dinner. Guilt hangs its head while the police officer writes a speeding ticket on the highway shoulder. Guilt punctuates the revelation of an illicit sexual affair. In its healthiest manifestation, guilt seeks to make things right. It recognizes that actions are able to hurt others. Apologies will follow. The aftermath of guilt is qualitatively different from shame. Shame lingers, tainting personal worth and acceptability. But the guilty, once forgiven, experience more immediate freedom. This does not mean the experience is forgotten. The sequence of guilt and forgiveness may indicate a different course of future action based on lessons learned. Guilt probably lives beneath Tina's reference to situations where adversaries picked on vulnerable children. Her statement likely recalls an episode where she remained on the sidelines, witnessing the exploitation of others when intervention was a valid option. Taken together, 'negative' moral emotions of shame and guilt marshal considerable influence over everyday experience.[18]

Shame and guilt are inversely related to the 'positive' moral emotion of pride. Pride is composed of two elements. Alpha pride is the opposite of shame. Alpha pride bestows fundamental worth upon the self. Beta pride is the opposite of guilt, referencing behaviors in a positive light. Both are evident in Annabelle's mealtime epiphany. Beta pride marks her achievement with fork, spoon, and spaghetti. Her immediate feelings are focused on the success of mealtime independence. The achievement becomes a trophy in Annabelle's subsequent exclamation – 'Look!' This matures into alpha pride directed toward the self. It is quickly evident that her achievement isn't limited to mealtimes. Knowledge of her success opens the door to other possibilities. Annabelle's sense of self is affirmed and nurtured through a net gain in confidence. This confidence might spill over into greater independence when she dresses in the morning or helps others put away the groceries. Not incidentally, these same processes happen for Tina, who stands next to Annabelle at the lunch table. Annabelle's feelings become Tina's feelings. L'Arche facilitates shared experience associated with deeply personal struggle to overcome shame and guilt.

The moral implications of shame, guilt, and pride are widely known in developmental psychology. Several moral emotion studies are focused on empathic behavior, an important aspect of maturity in compassionate love. As it turns out, individuals steeped in shame tend to demonstrate a strangely selfish kind of empathy. While caring remains the main objective, it is directed toward the needs of the *caregiver* rather than the recipient. A telling example comes from the research of June Tangney. A shamed research participant loudly exclaimed, 'It hurts *me* so much to see this happen to you!' Interestingly, guilt promotes empathy directed toward the needs of others. Guilt encourages the alignment of shared feelings between caregiver and recipient. It becomes much easier to care for others when the caregiver effectively understands human actions which hurt the care recipient. Tina's narrative at the beginning of the chapter reflects this kind of shared feeling. Ironically enough, her movement away from shame involves a measure of guilt which equips her to understand the nature of core member experience.

Guilt is clearly a better moral emotion than shame, especially when the former is accompanied by moderate levels of alpha and beta pride. Research suggests, however, that empathy is less likely when single moral emotions are manifested in the relative absence of others. Overwhelmed by shame, Tina is unable to care for herself, much less for others. Without the counterweight of pride, excessive guilt compels individuals to play safe and avoid helping others. Too much pride is perhaps even more problematic. Unchecked by the needs of others, pride leads to narcissism or, worse, sociopathy. Tina's movement from shame into moral maturity doesn't eliminate one moral emotion in favor of others. Without knowledge of shame, Tina is unable to identify with the needs of core members. Lacking basic guilt, Tina cannot understand forgiveness and receptivity. In the absence of pride, Tina is prevented from extending compassionate love to others in her community. Tina's journey indicates a reshuffling of moral emotions into dynamic balance, tempered and polished through the living example of core members such as Annabelle.

What causes these reshuffled moral emotions to stick in their new positions? Tina's story carries a hidden curriculum. Moral emotions like shame come to structure the way in which Tina perceives social situations requiring compassion, love, and forgiveness. But this can change. Even better, the change can become deeply entrenched with time. Over years spent in L'Arche, Tina is able to see that others (specifically core members) also experience shame. Shame gradually yields to a more balanced combination of emotions including guilt and pride. Change happens when Tina observes core members wrestling with similar issues. During these episodes, she experiences new combinations of moral emotions which are subsequently recorded in memory. These might be recalled during similar situations in the future, particularly where Tina is challenged to grow and mature. Reshuffled moral emotions help Tina to view herself differently. Instead of paralysing shame, she is able to recognize goodness in herself and others. Rather than living as a chronic outsider, Tina begins to engage others freely – no longer bound to external judgements of unworthiness or ugliness. Healing happens where shame moves away from the center of her emotional universe, replaced by receptivity, forgiveness, and the potential for compassionate love.

*   *   *

It is the weekend following our interview. Tina and I are walking the aisles of a local supermarket with Stacy, a core member first introduced through the indefatigable Amigo. We're having good fun. Tina removes items from the shelf and palms them like a basketball. After updating her list, she tosses each object to me as a forward pass. I subsequently hand items to Stacy, who crowds the cart like a player at the opposition basket, spiking boxes and cans with Olympic panache. Slam-dunk shopping. Patrons are giving us a wide berth, although several chuckle audibly at our antics. Tina and Stacy are giggling loudly. The atmosphere is carefree and ripe for practical jokes. Arching her eyebrows, Stacy initiates a flat tire campaign on Tina. Walking closely behind the assistant, Stacy tries to snag the heel of Tina's running shoes with the toe of her own shoe. The reward is a soft popping sound as Tina's foot bursts out of its shoe. Things rapidly escalate as the two women hop and shuffle on the industrial linoleum, each trying to gain the advantage on the opponent's shoe.

The shopping cart is jammed full as we join a queue near the storefront. Stacy closely studies chewing gum in a rack next to waiting shoppers. She looks up at Tina. The assistant nods and smiles. Stacy enthusiastically reaches for the gum, tearing open the package and handing out pieces. She is a model of charity. Half a dozen shoppers in our queue are approached with a gum offering. Many accept. While this is happening, an elderly woman taps me on the shoulder. Watching Stacy pass gum to a college student, she whispers that her youngest brother was developmentally disabled. Consistent with the expectations and practices of postwar America, the family institutionalized him. The woman is delighted that Stacy avoids this fate. We chat about societal and cultural changes which publicly welcome the disabled. While we talk, I am struck by the fact that such changes are unfolding right before my eyes. Stacy's activities speak loudly to the role of L'Arche in making an inclusive world for all God's people.

It is our turn with the supermarket employee who checks merchandise. The checker is visibly uncomfortable with Stacy's appearance. He offers polite greeting to Tina and myself, pointedly ignoring Stacy. All smiles are gone. Tina shifts on her feet, anxiously stealing glances at Stacy. After interminable seconds, Tina invites Stacy to the podium for the credit card swipe. The move is intended to include Stacy centrally in the checkout process despite the checker's behavior. Fully aware of what is happening, Stacy approaches the podium. Her unblinking gaze is fixed on the checker. With a small grunt, Stacy pulls a piece of chewing gum from her package. She hands it to the checker with an enormous, gap-toothed smile. The checker pauses and quickly accepts the gum without making eye contact. We are astonished. Stacy's absolute refusal to accept public shame is an extraordinary display of human resiliency. We push our cart through the electric doors into the parking lot. The sun peeks from between drifting cumulus. Stacy enthusiastically chomps on her gum. Her step is light.

*   *   *

New goals, different me

Up to this point, our discussion considers movement from shame to moral maturity through unconscious processes. But this does not reflect the entirety of Tina's story. Her narrative ends powerfully, demonstrating fully conscious awareness of her journey and its implications.

> I think the community allows people to be free. It's a movement into more freedom, more joy. More peace, more tolerance for other people. I get less worried about things now. I've always said God will provide, but now I'm living in it more.

Her comments are a testimonial to personal healing through freedom from shame. Compassionate love grows best when people seek things like joy, peace, and tolerance. Tina acquires a revised list of personal goals applicable for community living. These goals frame the manner by which she defines herself and the prerogatives of L'Arche. How do moral intuitions and emotions contribute to revised goals and priorities for the self?

Moral intuitions and emotions pack a considerable punch, yet they go about their business with the subtlety of everyday routine and habit. Tina's story suggests that, over long periods of time, changing habits can result in big alterations to identity or *moral self*. Previously alone, Tina now lives in the center of a vibrant community. Once paralysed by self-hatred, today she demonstrates empathy toward others through receptivity, forgiveness, and compassion. Movements in Tina's intuitive and emotional understanding of goodness shape her sense of self. The reshuffling of shame, guilt, and pride requires many rounds in a card game where other players similarly contend with disability and personal suffering. After several years in L'Arche, Tina sees something different when looking at herself in the mirror. New clothes accentuate beauty rather than homeliness. Mistakes are worthy of a laugh instead of condemnation. Forgiveness is an option where avoidance once reigned. Tina repeatedly encounters social situations engaging habits which pull her away from shame toward compassionate love of self and other.

Tina's movement from shame to moral maturity is marked by experiences influenced by revised moral intuitions and emotions. At some point she becomes aware of these changes, particularly as they are mirrored back through relationships with others. Her self-story begins to shift. Shame is slowly replaced by receptivity and forgiveness in self-understanding. New goals emerge in step with the priorities of the community, including things like joy, peace, and tolerance. Without a doubt, these goals reflect the Roman Catholic context of L'Arche. They are goals given to the religious and moral liberation of a people who understand suffering and marginalization. The importance of relationships in this process cannot be overlooked. Moral exemplars from Colby's and Damon's research point to the influence of key relationships in the formation of personal goals associated with humanitarian commitments.[19] One exemplar from the project recounts how a mentor teacher inspired her to adopt a new suite of personal goals associated with learning disabled children. Mentors for Colby's and Damon's exemplars are analogous to core member 'prophets' and 'teachers', offering a different vision of maturity. Much like Tina, the exemplar is not fully aware of mentor influence and revised goals until the significant passage of time. The years afford her with numerous experiences of self, framed by revised personal goals, across a variety of social circumstances.

This interpretation of Tina's developmental process runs deep into human biology. People behave in ways related to personal goals reflecting a moral self. This is colorfully illustrated through an obscure chapter in

American medical history. The renowned neurologist Antonio Damasio retells the sad tale of Phineas Gage, a 26-year-old railroad foreman in nineteenth-century New England.[20] Gage was lauded by his men as a conscientious boss and devoted family man. Among other talents, he was recognized as an expert with hard-rock blasting. Often Gage would help grade the rough-hewn railway with small, controlled explosions to dislodge natural barriers. He carried a special tamping iron for this purpose. Small holes were bored into rock and filled with blasting powder. Prior to ignition, Gage would use his iron to pack the powder tightly into the hole. In this way, the intended explosion was directed downward into the obstruction rather than upward toward the surface.

One unfortunate afternoon, Gage accidentally struck flint while packing blast powder into a railway hole. The explosive result was dramatic and gruesome. The iron rod was propelled upward like a missile, striking Gage beneath the left cheekbone and exiting through a small hole in the top of his head. Incredibly, he remained conscious and sought medical attention. He was able to talk with others and respond to questions. The ensuing infection was severe and nearly fatal. Despite his many challenges, Gage survived and appeared to regain normal health. Yet it became apparent that he was enormously changed because of the incident. Colleagues declared in unison that Gage was no longer the same person. He was unable to make effective decisions over matters of relational and financial significance. His work ethic, penchant for responsibility, and moral standards evaporated. He could not hold down a job or execute basic plans. His reputation for empathy and concern was replaced by disdain for others. Gage was newly insolent and profane in speech. He rapidly lost his fortune, leaving his wife and family for a directionless existence.

Damasio notes that Gage's injury was to a portion of the brain behind the eyes known as the *prefrontal cortex*. Social information is processed and regulated in the area. Damage to Gage's prefrontal cortex was particularly severe to structures involved in emotion and feeling. The absence of intuitive disgust and moral emotion is striking in the accounts of Gage's behavioral changes after the accident. Historical reconstruction of Gage's situation, however, is a poor substitute for contemporary study of similar injury with apparently moral implications. Damasio and his wife Hanna assembled a pool of neurological patients with brain damage much like Gage. These individuals carried similar records of impaired work performance, social responsibility, planning, and moral competence following their injuries. Importantly, all were hindered in their ability to articulate and realize personal goals. When given Kohlberg's MJI, however, patient responses were identical to a matched control group of individuals without brain damage. Thus the patients were entirely normal in their ability to understand and choose justice in Kohlberg's dilemmas. Yet without personal goals, these individuals struggled to behave virtuously, especially in dimensions of empathy, compassion, and caring in relationships.

Intuitions potentially inform emotions, which in turn scaffold personal goals associated with a moral self. This is an integrative process, the importance of which becomes evident through the tragic examples of Gage and Damasio's brain-damaged patients. When injury short-circuits an ability to experience moral emotions, the moral self becomes unhinged from its goals. Moral reasoning is unaffected, but compassionately moral behavior is hugely constricted. It happens that shame, guilt, and pride provide ongoing reinforcement for goals which define the self in its relationship with others. Consider Tina's mention of *tolerance*. Regular achievement of this goal requires past memory of emotions associated with difficult people doing unpleasant things. Tolerance isn't easy. It requires a willingness to look past the immediate behavior of others toward a better tomorrow. Tina's experience in L'Arche with difficult people teaches her that others sometimes wake up on the wrong side of the bed. They struggle with their own shame and suffering. Despite present appearances, difficult people should not be judged by the sum total of their actions. They are still beloved of God.

The loss of emotional memory makes regular achievement of the tolerance goal difficult for Gage and others suffering similar injury. But for Tina, these intact memories help keep her tolerance goal in clear focus. When confronted with an angry core member wielding a broom, she remembers past events and emotions which helped orient her moral self around tolerant and compassionate priorities. In the moment she takes a deep breath and weighs the past with her conviction that tolerance matters greatly, and that she is a tolerant person in the present. Moreover, she knows that she will be a tolerant person tomorrow, next week, and over the coming decade.[21] She asks the angry core member to sit down for some conversation. Rather than respond with fear or anger, Tina respects the potential issues behind the other's difficult behavior. The core member might have been provoked. He might have missed his medications. Something might have happened which reminded him of a past hurt. Tolerance means accepting people at face value. Through her invitation to sit and talk, Tina isn't concerned about whether she finds the root meaning of the man's behavior. She is concerned with his worth as a person. She cares enough to take time with his difficult feelings, even if the process of wading through them is distasteful.

*   *   *

It is my last day in the community. Tina is panicked. Her massive key ring is gone. Many of us join forces to help her find it. The keys, which access car and house, are fastened to a large ring. The ring is linked to a short golden chain. At the bottom of the chain dangles a panda bear amulet. Even more than keys, it is the potential loss of the bear amulet which fuels Tina's grief. The amulet is from China, keepsake from a treasured visit to that country some five years ago. After spending weeks in a remote village near Chengdu, the panda was presented as a gift from a 12-year-old girl. The girl lost her mother to disease. Tina became a kind of surrogate parent during her time in the village. Along with some pictures, the amulet is Tina's reminder of an important, if distant relationship. We scour the house for the keys. For more than an hour we pull cushions from the couch, rifle through paper stacks in the sunroom office, and comb the grass between car and house. Nothing. Tina is managing things well, but the wrinkles around her eyes are telling. Her usually sunny disposition is darkened.

We hear a shout from upstairs. A caregiver assistant named Leticia dangles lost keys from the upstairs landing. Tina runs upstairs while I go outside to call off the search. When I return, Tina is quietly conversing with Leticia in the hallway. Things are not right. Apparently the keys were found under a pillow. The pillow and bed belong to a core member named Brianne. It is clear to Leticia that the keys were carefully hidden sometime after the bed was made in the morning. From what I can tell, this is not the first time that Brianne furtively introduced herself to someone else's things. The assistants decide that a confrontation is necessary. The decision is made without frustration or rancor, but with considerable sadness. Wishing to respect the delicate nature of the situation, I elect to take a neighborhood walk. For half an hour I am gone. Outside the sky is overcast. Small droplets of rain are audible on the broad leaves of an enormous fern by the sidewalk. Cars and buses slide past with lights on against the coming twilight.

As I return to the house, I glance through the large bay window fronting the porch. Tina is sitting with Brianne on the living room sofa. The women are angled toward each other, hands clasped. From my

121

vantage it looks as if they are praying together. Brianne is weeping, tears coursing down her cheeks. Although I cannot hear the conversation, everything is clear. Along with the key ring, theft is right out on the table. The matter apparently does nothing to diminish Brianne's intrinsic worth – Tina speaks with tenderness and authentic concern for her friend. Yet the issue causes pain. Brianne recognizes this fact and atones with her deep sadness. Receptivity, forgiveness, and tolerance are palpable through the bay window. Even from this distance I am concerned about intruding on the moment. I think about retracing my steps and finding a back-door entry to the house. As I turn, I notice that Tina holds the key ring in her hand. She carefully unlinks the short golden chain from the main ring. She hands the panda bear amulet to Brianne. The two embrace as I walk back down the steps and into the rain.

*   *   *

Goal-corrected partnership

The fruit of Tina's transition from shame to moral maturity is her ability to trust others. Trust is finishing cement in the practice of compassionate love. Her ability to trust reflects a stable moral self, grounded upon personal goals reflecting a balanced cohort of moral emotions and intuitions. The proof is plainly visible through the bay window. Trust positions relationship above material priorities. Trust enables generosity. Trust encourages L'Arche core members and assistants to adopt the perspective of others, using that knowledge to compassionately loving ends. Perhaps unexpectedly, community members come to understand themselves better through this knowledge of others. It is much easier to trust when individuals know and trust themselves. Trust deepens when this knowledge includes others – the collective stakes are brought clearly into view. Tina is able to extend forgiveness and compassion to Brianne knowing the good woman's background, insecurities, and fears. The greatest exhibitions of compassionate love in L'Arche happen where pain is received with trust and validation rather than reaction and avoidance. Trust invokes security.

The great attachment theorist John Bowlby argued that trusting and secure children mature most rapidly when they come to appreciate what things are like for their parents. It is harder to throw a tantrum or create an argument when one understands the good intentions of another. Adopting the perspective of the other, children and parents are able to construct shared identities imbued with trust, security, and love. Not surprisingly, shared identities are built on shared goals. Bowlby called this process a *goal-corrected partnership*. True, child–parent relationships do not exist in L'Arche, but these communities function as families. The pictures in the sunroom office tell the story. Surrogate attachment relationships are part of the landscape. Elements of Bowlby's insight are visible through Tina's growth detailed in this chapter. In L'Arche, movement away from shame anticipates a moral maturity characterized by secure and trustworthy commitments. Shared identities flourish. Annabelle and Tina share a common identity of empowerment, built on shared goals of perseverance and fortitude. Goal-corrected partnerships reflect give-and-take. With time, Tina's personal goals are refashioned on the basis of partnerships with other assistants and core members, both past and present. In the case of L'Arche, these goal-corrected partnerships elicit new possibilities for relationship and healing – opportunities characterized by compassionate love.

My bag is packed. Tina, Stacy, and I are sharing farewells on the front stoop. This is the last American L'Arche community I will visit on the research grant. The funding is exhausted and a mound of data awaits my full attention. Amigo stands next to Stacy, tail slowly fanning the morning air. Tina taps her forehead as if remembering a nearly forgotten tidbit. She says that the interview helped clarify important milestones in her experience. Mulling the questions over these past few days, she realizes an omission. Her journey of healing critically involves a core member relationship with Gene. He is now passed away. Tina's memory of this gentleman lives powerfully, if only because of what he taught her about freedom and maturity in L'Arche.

I was living at another L'Arche home about eight years ago. That's when the magnitude of the changes inside really began to hit me. There was a core member in that home named Gene. He had really intense emotional problems. When you look at his life, it is amazing that he was alive at all. His background could've been the script for a horror movie. I am amazed that he was able to smile. He had an unusual behavior that he 'shared' with almost everyone at some point. [ruefully smiles, uses fingers to make quotation marks] He and I were sitting on the porch talking and he picked up this big stick and threatened to beat me with it. He was very serious. He had done that in the past with other people – it was one of his coping patterns. He was more likely to behave that way when under stress. There were a lot of stressful things happening in the house at that particular time.

I looked closely at his face. Just like that, it changed. [snapping fingers] He had the sweetest eyes and a great smile and all of a sudden I was looking at a different person. I can't describe it very well, but his eyes went hard and dark and you could tell he wasn't himself any more. It was like his internal demons were right on the surface. When I saw that shift in him, I knew what to expect. Everybody who worked at that particular L'Arche house was given background information about Gene. It was important for personal safety to understand him. You must understand the kind of the things that he was dealing with, and so I was already on guard. I was watching for signals and triggers and that sort of thing, but mainly looking for changes in his face.

There's a kind of syndrome which comes with vigilance. I saw it with other assistants; I felt it myself. When you lived in this particular home, Gene got mad at you on a regular basis. You began to think in terms of what I could do to keep him from feeling this way. How could I change to keep from triggering him? What did I do wrong this time to make him mad? You were constantly on guard. You began to deal with things as though they happened because of simple cause and effect. My action caused his reaction. When you watched his face do that for the first time, you begin to get it. You realize this is not about me. You might have realized this before, but you didn't. It really kicks you in the head, tells you a lot about relationships, trust, and L'Arche. Gene's stuff is much bigger than you. It seems almost silly that you didn't realize it before; he is dealing with something huge. It is not about what you just did. It is not about the fact that you asked him to take his medicine. It is not about the fact that you wouldn't give him snuff. Once you get to this point, it is only a short step to a bigger awareness, a larger maturity. We have a tendency to think about our-selves first because that is the only person we understand, or so we think. But we only know ourselves because of others. It puts you in a different mindset of wow, it is not about me. Ego with a capital 'E' starts to melt down a little bit. At least it did for me. That is the first step to becoming a lot of those ideals that I told you about. Things like receptivity, forgiveness, and acceptance. Once you understand that L'Arche is not just about you, it gives you a lot of understanding of what it really is about. L'Arche is about shared goals like love and tolerance. It is about freedom to live in a place where the best and worst parts of each person are tolerated or, better yet, embraced.

6

Road to Guadalupe

These are words, but they have a very deep meaning. Trust, hope, but even deeper than these things. Deep to all your surroundings and relationship with God. You try to put each word in your daily life and live everything around that word.

(Nicholas, a 40-year-old L'Arche assistant)

It's a birthday party! The sun is setting in the cloudless western sky. The wall thermometer is pegged above 90 degrees. A back-yard affair, the entire L'Arche community is busily preparing for celebration. Sayid is at the grill flipping burgers. Cherise sets out potato salad, fruit, chips, and soda. Core members Lillian and James are filling water balloons with the assistance of Lawrence, a long-term assistant. Other community members come and go, cheerfully looking after birthday chores. The air is mildly electric with anticipation over the gathering, to include several dozen residents from other L'Arche homes a short walk away. Katarina was born on this day 51 years ago. She is one of the most difficult core members in the American L'Arche zone. Institutionalized for decades, Katarina is capable of explosive anger and terrible tantrums. Yet an outsider would have no inkling of her reputation. Lillian and Lawrence discuss how much the good woman enjoys an old-fashioned water balloon war. Cherise prominently displays Katarina's favorite soda purchased on an insider's tip. Sayid tells me that he's making double cheeseburgers, a Katarina special. For her part Katarina offers a quiet contribution – meticulously raking the lawn which is barren of leaves. Long hair hangs low over her stooped figure. In the twilight I catch a glimpse of her face. She is radiant.

I am struck by the inclusive attitude of the group. As newcomers arrive there are great shouts of greeting, laughter, and hugs. Without warning I am swept into the festivities like a beloved relative from a distant coast. Perceiving that people are hungry, Sayid summons everyone (now numbering more than 40 people) to form a circle holding hands. We sing a prayer and line up with plates and cutlery alongside the dinner tables. Nancy (a caregiver assistant) tilts her head, offering commentary regarding the scene and its deeper meaning.

> L'Arche is a small thing, you know. We serve 13 people with disabilities and there are thousands in our city alone. We know we are not a solution and I am not helping that many people. I am not doing anything great. I am doing something small – I do the dishes, I cook a meal, I take them to a doctor appointment, and I help a very small amount of people. We are a sign of hope and not a solution, we are not really solving anything. We are kind of living life small and helping a few people but mostly it is remarkable because we love each other. You know, I am never going to be known for this or get money from it but it has been the best thing in my life thus far.

L'Arche redeems difficult hope. These communities celebrate people as a matter of habit, capturing what is best about each individual and shamelessly parading its value. The back-yard harbors implicit recognition of Katarina's personal struggles and difficult behaviors. Core members and assistants know that the party atmosphere could be shattered in a moment by fits of rage. Yet instead of casting a pall over the gathering, this knowledge is liberating. L'Arche recognizes that all are disabled but nevertheless worthy of dignity and unrestrained respect. This knowledge is safe, compassionate, and tender. It is a sign of hope.

Hope is the gift of disability to moral maturity.[1] My purpose in this chapter is to explore how hope is learned and experienced through the practice of compassionate love in L'Arche. As before, our main source of instruction will be the stories which are the people of L'Arche. These stories will help us understand how hope nurtures *moral character* or aspects of mature self given to the flourishing of others in love. With a nod to contemporary scientific research on character, the stories are organized on the basis of four core themes including *redemption, agency, helpers and enemies*, and *communion*. These themes are applied from recent work by an expert on the topic, with summary discussion added from an earlier project I published on assistant goals. L'Arche is an incubator for loving character, celebrating life in the midst of disability. Caregiver assistants come to understand their own disabilities even as these are hidden from external view. With this wisdom comes hope of reconciliation and healing which pushes individuals more deeply into the practice of compassionate love.

Hoping for character

Despite the warmth of the back-yard scene, I am not suggesting that Katarina is fully arrived. She is no Pollyanna. Consistent with nearly every face around the party circle, Katarina is under construction. Compassionate love does its work slowly with little regard for deadlines. Katarina is in the midst of ongoing change – a process of development. The wonder of the birthday party is that she is unilaterally accepted without amendments, conditions, or promises. In the absence of hope, such affirmation is impossible. The celebration is about Katarina becoming more of her authentic self rather than a former persona left to rot in the mental institution. The hope embedded in birthday salutations is that she is of great worth – her development in L'Arche renews the same potential for others. Through the developmental example furnished by disabled core members, assistants are confronted both with personal limitations and unequivocal worth. While at times painful, embrace of these unlikely bedfellows is loudly celebrated by the community just as for Katarina. The people of L'Arche learn a more substantial hope in these moments, which over time is forged into moral maturity of durable character.

What is character and how is it nurtured by hope? Scores of philosophers and theologians have struggled with this question over many centuries. Without disparaging their good efforts, it is worth noting that the character issue is a major concern in scientific research.[2] A leader in the area is Lawrence J. Walker at the University of British Columbia. Walker reports data suggesting that character is partly related to the development of coherent identity or sense of self associated with moral priorities and commitments. With his colleagues, Walker demonstrated that narrative identities of persons widely perceived as morally mature share five core themes. These include *redemption, agency,* the presence of *helpers and enemies, communion,* and *attachment.*[3] We have already considered attachment as a discussion point in Chapter 4. The remaining themes are evident in caregiver assistant narratives, particularly those reflecting on hope in L'Arche. I have organized assistant stories following a brief introduction of each of the remaining themes. Although their stories are often situated beyond L'Arche, assistants report a common process of growth and reflection with the encouragement of core members like Katarina. A significant part of assistant maturing in the practice of compassionate love involves a return to painful periods of suffering and brokenness in order to construct meaning. Resulting wisdom is driven by hope, the validation of essential human worth in moral character.

Redemption

Walker's emphasis on redemption in moral character development takes cues from the familiar work of Dan McAdams at Northwestern University. *Redemption* refers to the reclamation of good from difficult circumstances. To put it bluntly, character is revealed in the individual's ability to make lemonade out of lemons – redeeming the underlying meaning of apparently hopeless situations. Morally mature individuals in Walker's study insisted that the worst circumstances are overcome not by raw willpower or blind perseverance, but through a measured conviction that greater possibilities are knocking at the door. It is perhaps no surprise that the redemption theme often coincides with spiritual and religious allusions. In L'Arche, assistant narratives commonly invoke biblical imagery of persons enduring the bad for the sake of the good. Examples are common. In the Old Testament, Abraham and Sarah are redeemed from decades of childlessness prior to the conception and birth of Isaac. In the New Testament, St Paul is redeemed on the Damascus road following his bitter persecution of the early church. Redemption involves effort to find the cloud's silver lining while recognizing that circumstances are potentially larger than humanly perceived horizons. Redemption runs on hope and lives for gratitude, compassion, forgiveness, and love. It is realized with hindsight, often to the surprise of assistants who found themselves instructed by the profundity of their own experiences.

* * *

Melanie is 55 years old, a recently arrived caregiver assistant in L'Arche. She is graying, with a penchant for large earrings. Our interview breaks new ground. We are seated at opposing ends of a see-saw in a neighborhood park near her L'Arche home. The park is the only quiet option for an active household with loudly vocalizing core members. Earlier rains have left the park benches soaked and we are making the best of it. The recorder is precariously balanced in the middle of the see-saw. Red, orange, and yellow maple leaves are slowly falling around us, adding to a thick carpet on the sodden ground.

> Back in the early 1990s I considered suicide. It all shook down over my 14-year-old son. He was a runaway and I was searching for him. In the state of Montana it is not illegal to run away. So I would go out at night looking for him. I was ready to drive myself up a pole. At that

time, however delusional or irrational or erroneous it might seem, my only value was this child and I couldn't even get that right. I was one of those people you would never think is struggling with suicide. I have always been a Disneyland Christian. Everything is good and beautiful and there is no Satan, there is nobody dark. It is all good and light. I still prefer to live that way. Depression was foreign to me because I always thought you have to have hope. But now I was in that place where I could understand how bad things could look, the darkness of the soul. One of the biggest lessons which came out of that is that my identity is not based on another human being. No matter how much I love that person. No matter how much I wanted to see them saved from their despair. That wasn't my job to do. I wasn't going to be able to fix this one.

I think in some way I wanted God to save Michael's life – really, what was left of my life now was God's. You see, I was a single parent. I never dated while my son was growing up, I was too busy working and driving to soccer games and basketball games. What I am saying is that he was my life, this child. So when his life blew up, my identity went with it. This was kind of scary and of course I know this is a very unhealthy thing. In L'Arche all of that is so valuable because now I am with core members who have lost it; they are mad, angry, throwing things. Can I for that moment go back to realizing that I am no different? All the things we bring with us to L'Arche, however bad or ugly they are, they are of value now.

*   *   *

Trevor is 36 years old with a thick shock of blond hair and lucid blue eyes. He is from Wales, with a lovely Cardiff accent. We are conversing in the laundry room of his home. Although I am initially reluctant to conduct an interview in this location, the white noise of a humming dryer offers Trevor a greater sense of privacy. He is engaged to Michelle, an assistant introduced in Chapter 3. One on one, Trevor reveals a tender side that balances his famously sarcastic wit.

My mum recently died of Alzheimer's. It was a tragic thing, but it was more like the moment of mourning my mum's death eight years after she had died. It was something that moved mountains deep within me. In L'Arche, I don't know if anyone has told you – we have *accompaniers*, usually people who have been in L'Arche a long time. They are like mentors. I remember saying to my accompanier that most of my peers have parents who are still living. Because of this, I felt like an outsider. The whole experience of death is very much related to L'Arche because downward mobility is a lot of dying to anything that previously had value. So my mum was diagnosed with Alzheimer's and lived for quite a few years. I remember calling my accompanier on the phone and she said, 'The most important part of L'Arche is to accompany people to their death.' Ultimately, Robert [core member] gave me one of the most profound gifts since I came to L'Arche. Something happened a couple of days before he went into the hospital. It was a bright Saturday morning and I woke him up, and he looked at me. This was only a week or two before he died. Robert looks at me and goes, 'Jesus is in heaven and he talks a lot.' So I said to Robert, 'What's he saying to you?' He said, 'He has many packages for me.'

There's a line out of *Tuesdays with Morrie*, I don't know if you have ever read it, where the narrator says, 'When you learn how to die you learn how to live.'[4] My mum knew she would die very young. It was known and she accepted it. Robert knew also. I believe Robert didn't die earlier this year because he didn't know if the [L'Arche] house could sustain it. I honestly think he and God had a conversation in which it was decided. He knew and he blessed a lot of people with his knowledge. Life is so circular in L'Arche – it is about helping the folks through. They have died so many times in their lives over certain things that we haven't. I think it takes an acceptance of walking in their shoes. It is easy to get mad at the core members or not be patient, but I just pray that I am patient because I know their pain has got to be great.

*   *   *

Natalie is 49 years old, with hazel eyes and skin wizened by long exposure to the sun. The corners of her mouth are perpetually curled up, intimating a keen sense of irony. She is impeccably dressed in a dark wool suit and pumps. Natalie explains that she was asked to make a presentation on behalf of the regional L'Arche network to a private foundation. The presentation just preceded our interview and she is awash in adrenaline. Natalie is former director of the network. I sense that she is relieved to have handed the baton to others. I soon find out why.

I was director and we had a process we were going through to come up
with a new mandate. I've led discernment processes and have been
through them. Now it was my turn to lead the discernment process to
choose a new coordinator. [In L'Arche, *mandates* and *discernment* can
relate to the development of community vision statements and, at
times, selection of key staff.] That was intimidating but great. I knew
in my gut how to do it and how it should look. Anyway, the process
for our community was to come up with a mandate and then the next
month we'd go through a discernment. We'd had a rough year with
one of the homes and the team there. They had gotten separated from
the rest of the community. It was kind of like the cancer that you can't
name but you know there's a lot of confusion. It's hard to articulate –
it's that dark part in our world. When you feel a lot of confusion and
can't articulate things, you know it's not right.

I and the rest of the coordinating team got pummeled in it. The
board didn't stand up and say, 'This isn't right.' I think it was because
people weren't able to articulate it and they were saying, 'Oh really?'
I felt completely betrayed by the community and people on the board.
We were starting on Friday night and it didn't feel right. I could see
what was happening. I said to the discernment team, 'This isn't right.
What we've been told to do needed to stop. This process isn't a discernment process.' It was so bad that it was almost funny. Except my
soul was exposed. It was horrid. It was the hardest thing I'd ever lived
through. At least that's how I took it. I cried for three days straight. It
was like someone died! My heart was broken. There was a part of me
that was dead. Over the next few days I thought about whether to
resign as director.

The discernment team finished that weekend, and the coordinating
team; we had no authority after that. It was so ugly and hard and
yucky. After those people left a few months later things were better.
But I stayed with it. It was really painful. At one point I met with my
spiritual director and laid everything out on the table. I thought,
'How can I kill myself?' That's not me. Whoa. I stayed with it for ten
or twelve months. What I'm living now is the grace from that difficult
time. It's been great that I stayed another year. Then I ended up
leaving really well. What I'm learning, it's the mystery . . . is to look at
what is the light of God. You're going through the tunnel of darkness
but there's light that will come from that. The whole mystery of what
will come from that. It's the faith that keeps deepening in me. You've

got to stay with it. Don't run from it. Don't run to substances. I was grateful to the community.

At one point I said to Christopher Price [board member], 'It doesn't feel like you're supporting me.' There were issues there. Christopher said, 'You're like the daughter I never had.' [tearful] It was really joyous; it was great being with the core members, with Daniela. She lived with us for three years and then she had to go into the institution because she was psychotic. She had a mental illness and a developmental disability. Huge psychotic break and it was really hard. She died a couple of years ago. What I'm trying to articulate is the contentment. Up until I became director my life was so encompassed in L'Arche. We have a life outside L'Arche, but the essence of our life is in L'Arche. The fruit of the struggle was contentment.

*   *   *

Redemption is difficult. It commonly traces hope in terms of faith, incorporating images of the journey, darkness, and light associated with God. Together the stories illustrate a redemptive experience where hope presses through desolation toward greater understanding of one's place in relationships and the world.[5] Love grows deeper as a result. The narratives are deeply emotional, not just in content but through the real-time experience of telling stories. Shame and hurt are abundantly evident in Natalie's reference to soul 'exposure' joined with feelings of betrayal and isolation. Trevor's recollections are saturated in grief. The searing picture of Melanie's quest to find her son is filled with anxiety and desperation. During the interview, assistants struggled to articulate their thoughts clearly for pain retrieved in memory. Yet the redemptive element is unmistakable. Core members are prominent in redemption. Daniela and Robert are palpable reminders of a hopeful vision for God's greater purposes in human affairs. This purpose is animated by compassionate love.

The stories richly document moral character in assistant development. In all three instances assistants personally (and unexpectedly) thanked me for the interview. When I asked why, the response was so uncannily similar that it might have been scripted by a hidden director. *Telling my story reminds me why I am in L'Arche and why my life matters.* This is the same pattern found in Walker's research, namely that redemptive meaning reflects a stable, consistent sense of self aligned with fundamental moral priorities. The recognition of those priorities is liberating and of enormous value. For assistants, mature character is all about the moral vision of L'Arche. It is unwavering commitment to the essential value of humanity without regard to mental or physical capacity. Caregiver assistants demonstrate a reordered understanding of relationships and the moral force of core members who model hope. The weld points on their narrative identities are deeply emotional, reflecting the gravity of desperate times redeemed in the context of intimate relationships.[6]

Agency

Walker's project on character highlights *agency* as a recurring theme in narrative identities of the morally mature. First noted in McAdams, the agency motif quashes any notion of character as spineless. Agency involves proper and ethical use of power, mastery, and achievement.[7] More often than not, it surfaces through fidelity to personal values that precede the practice of compassionate love. To have agency in L'Arche doesn't require a competitive spirit. Rather, people must be interested in making a difference; leaving a mark of hope or advocacy that changes the status quo. Not surprisingly, agency is related to the notion of generativity discussed in Chapter 4. Agency is readily observed in L'Arche assistants who recognize the world's unfairness and refuse to take things lying down. Hope in this sense should be understood as an active rather than a passive posture. Agency realizes a vision of compassionate love that is full and dynamic, reaching into every corner of human experience. L'Arche makes for an interesting cross-section of agency observation in narrative reflections. The following stories range far and wide, with several noteworthy similarities.

*   *   *

Maria is 57 years old and widowed. She is a tiny woman from a migrant farming community in the San Joaquin Valley of Central California. With pride she tells me that her hometown is the traditional setting for Steinbeck's epic novel *The Grapes of Wrath*. Maria's work-roughened hands are neatly folded in her lap. She is the epitome of Old World dignity and manners. Right now, we are sipping tea in the kitchen of her L'Arche home. The furnishings are simple and worn, the linoleum scuffed, and the room spotlessly clean for guests. Maria's story is measured and deliberate. Her eyes smolder with quiet strength.

Twenty years ago I had three kids, no child support. I was depressed. I once heard a psychology professor say that you don't have to go through a deep depression to know how it feels to be sad. I wanted to stop that teacher to say that you do! You can't understand what it feels like to miscarry if it's never happened to you. To go through a deep depression . . . remember that one book, they did a movie on it. *Girl, Interrupted.*[8] We had to write a paper on it. She talks about this thin membrane that separates people with disorders. She would cross through that membrane and then come back. The deep dark feeling that goes with it, you can't describe it. I had to share the movie with my best friend so he'd know that I'm more predisposed to depression. I have to be really careful. If things are stressful I have to get out. I have to back out and say, 'These are my boundaries. I can't do this, I need to take some time.' Back when my three kids were home, I had no furniture. I had no money, couldn't work, and was trying to get state support. I wanted to go back to school – they wouldn't accept work experience any more. My mom was sending $25 a week. I was cutting coupons out of the newspaper to get Tony's pizzas. The baby had lots of health problems, she was lactose allergic. She couldn't digest things. Her formula alone was $250 per month. My mom was sending money for rent, my grandfather too . . . everyone was trying to help me. The despair was overwhelming – the feeling of worthlessness. I can't make enough money to pay for childcare.

The first time I went to the welfare office to get help, I went in and they basically laughed at me. It was terrible. I was crying. 'You're supposed to get $1,500 per month, what is your problem?' But I'm not getting it! They said, 'Your vehicle is worth too much, you need to sell your vehicle, you need to file bankruptcy, you need to be evicted from your duplex.' They were looking at me and laughing. I was mortified. I was looking at the people around me and thinking I was above this. Then I went through a huge metamorphosis; went through this deep depression and came out of it. [eyes burning] I went back to the welfare office a second time and realized the people were just like me. I realized they were no different, just in different situations. I realized that these people were in terrible situations beyond their control. So I said to myself, 'I will wait all day to get what I deserve.' I filed for bankruptcy, I sold my vehicle and I moved to a cheaper place. 'Give me my papers and give me my support now.' It changed me in the way of being more assertive. I deserved this, there was no reason I shouldn't get it. Whatever I need to do, tell me and I'll do it.

Being able to see people differently. I was almost ashamed of myself for the attitudes I used to have. Why did I think that I was any different? I'm no different. We're just different people. Coming into L'Arche, it's this same acceptance. L'Arche does incredible things to make a life with a handful of resources. Making it work, that's what is incredible.

*   *   *

Joy is 38 years old. She is of average height with wavy brown hair cut at shoulder length. She is dressed L'Arche – meaning that casual comfort is the order of the day. We are chatting in the old parlor room of her L'Arche Victorian home in the Eastern United States. Despite ageing furniture and peeling wallpaper, the place is still grand. Our voices echo in the narrow room with high ceiling and gingerbread crown molding. Joy is a positive individual who grew up in trying circumstances. Our conversation is frank and direct. Deep faith is liberally sprinkled throughout her narrative.

I was in counseling and had to accept my role in an abusive relationship that I couldn't accept before. He's the asshole, he's the one. When I accepted the fact that I chose to be there, I had warning signs that were practically knocking me over the head. I chose it, I chose to be there, I chose to interact with all those situations and it was my responsibility for my life. I started praying for him too. One night I said, 'I need to pray for him.' My daughter couldn't believe it. The only way to let go of it is to let it be God's. Just like the wrongness of capital punishment, it's not our job to punish people. It's our job to do what we can do with our lives. We're only in charge of our own lives. Our own selves. I'm choosing something. I call it 'acceptance'.

I have to remind myself all the time when I'm stressed out that I chose L'Arche, nobody's keeping me here, at any moment I could say to Keith [L'Arche director for this city] that I need to leave. It's my choice. I told him what I needed, to go part-time. That's also my choice. I want to continue part-time, but I have other needs financially. He respects it. I know that he values my work here, he's told me that. That's priceless. To have the director say, 'I want you to be here. I value what you do.' I took a week off in April, and he said, 'Whatever you need, Joy.' We all make choices, so I bring myself back to that. I have no control over anyone else. This hugely relates not only to L'Arche, but to my entire life. Every day I have to remind myself that it's my choice. How do I choose to start my day? Sometimes I choose to start bad, I'm in a bad mood and I want to go with it! Then I have to laugh at myself and say I chose to be crabby all day. We all chose to be here. We can choose to make it work or we can choose to fight with each other or be unhappy. It's our choice. Sometimes people choose without choosing. You let someone else choose for you. I choose life.

*   *   *

Andrew is 30 years old. Raised in a small town on the Great Plains, he delights in telling me about the wonders of city life. Like many L'Arche communities, Andrew's home is located in an older neighborhood where housing is comparatively affordable. The area around this home is hip, a source of perpetual interest for Andrew, who loves coffee houses. He is single and once studied for the priesthood. In his words, L'Arche is 'the right fit'. We are talking in Andrew's bedroom, a sometimes quiet place. In the distance we can hear the vocalizations of a core member resident.

I was at a L'Arche renewal in Ireland and part of that was an eight-day directed retreat. During the retreat they asked us to be silent the whole time. I had my retreat all planned out before it started. I was going to read all through my notes; it was at the end of the six-week renewal. So I was going to read my renewal notes and I had some books I wanted to read and mapped out how I was going to use my time. The first night we were gathered around; one person from the retreat team issued the invitation to enter this week with no books. Everything in me just screamed, no, no, no – my controlling part. Something deep inside me wanted to accept that invitation although I knew it was going to be hard. I made a deep interior choice to say 'Yes' to that and when I did there was a peace that came over. That moment was the letting go of control.

So each morning after breakfast I would go sit in the library with my cup of coffee and I didn't have anything to do. I mean we were supposed to pray and stuff. So I would just sit there and say, 'OK God, what is new for today?' Do you know that each day of that retreat was walks in nature, times of prayer, each day was full. At one point during the retreat, they had this table with art materials and stuff and I went over and picked up some crayons and started drawing and was making lines on the page and everything. Then there were some watercolors so I kind of did this little watercolor. After they dried I put them up in my bedroom on the closet door. I had started the scribble with a red spiral in the middle and then I had taken some dark colors and went all over, but the gift of it was to see everything with the eyes of faith. We were asked a question at the beginning about seeing chaos and change as positive, that God is in the midst of what seems awful on the outside. So anyway, the high point of that retreat was seeing, experiencing, letting go of control. When I do that, I really experience the gifts of life that are available. So now I try to start every day with, 'God, what is today holding?' I still read every morning, but it is that desire to be open to what God has in store instead of what I think, I try to be open to whatever. Living in L'Arche, there are all kinds of challenges and shortages of assistants, and crises with core members. So it is seeing all of that, being able to see that with the eyes of faith and knowing that God is in it and seeing the gift in it.

*   *   *

Each assistant recounts situations associated with an understanding of self characterized by agency, empowered to cope with a chaotic world. Yet these stories are curiously different from popular expectations for achievement. None are boardroom testimonies for effective corporate leadership. We are not talking about lofty accomplishments directed toward fame or a secure and happy retirement. Instead, agency for these assistants is about finding hope in the midst of uncertain or even abusive circumstances. Often hope involves actions undertaken with or on behalf of others. These actions become a central feature in the development of self. Again and again, hope comes to roost in L'Arche. The kind of agency illustrated in these narratives is strikingly reminiscent of downward mobility, recognizing that disability and difficulties are assets toward the greater gift of knowing God's activities revealed in the community.

It is interesting to note the 'control' motif in narratives from Joy and Andrew. At face value, control is a classic feature of agency in moral character. The juxtaposition of control between the two narratives suggests a nuanced process of maturing. For Joy, control means choice – the option to leave an abusive relationship with the recognition that she is worthy and esteemed. For Andrew, control means taking initiative away from God. The notion is positive in Joy's narrative and negative in Andrew's.

Yet both are examples of agency. Taking control in Joy's world means reha-
bilitating self-worth with the same kind of respect and honor that we find
at Katarina's birthday party. Control takes charge of chaos in a manner
hopeful of a different future. In Andrew's case, relinquishment of control
to God is the means for handling disorder. This is the 'gift' returned after
the assistant recognizes his spiritual roadblock and then takes steps to
ameliorate it. Control in L'Arche is not about influencing others to
accomplish great things. There is no emphasis on pulling oneself up by
bootstraps. Instead we find acceptance – agency working through moral
character by affirming the essential value of individuals and relationships.
Each agent (Maria, Joy, Andrew) references his or her actions against a
larger community of valued human beings. It is this L'Arche community
rather than the individual agent which serves as the locus of change.

Helpers and enemies

Walker underlines a third theme in moral character expressed in terms of
helpers and enemies. The presence of helping individuals early in development coincides with a noted lack of enemies, or enemies who unwittingly
drove the morally mature into deeper moral commitments. Tutelage from
these helping mentors sparks a legacy of compassionate love passed on
between generations regardless of blood relation. In L'Arche, assistants
routinely talk about early helpers and their positive influence. Helpers are
sometimes identified in heroes or heroines from popular culture. More
often they are persons lacking notoriety in siblings, parents, friends,
coaches, teachers, or other mentor figures. Helpers provide tangible
reason to hope. They inspire and guide. Assistants note their influence
at the critical moments of life – during illness, addiction recovery, or
through relational transitions such as bereavement or divorce. Character
is shaped by an unseen cohort of people whose voices echo from the past.
During the interview phase of the research project, it was clear that each
assistant's account of compassionate love was a 'team effort', sculpted by
many other helpers who willingly invested in that individual's development. Interestingly, many assistants spontaneously associated the compassionate lessons of a core member in their lives with helpers from the past.
Core members provide a living link with mentoring helpers, strengthening the practice of love.

*   *   *

Susan is 60 years old and doesn't look 50. She wears jeans and Birken-
stocks with a fleece vest beneath dyed blonde hair. Susan is something of
a legend in L'Arche, known throughout the American zone as an impassioned advocate for the core members. We are seated in the living room of
her L'Arche home in the Midwest. Light snow is falling outside. It is late
morning and the core members are at day programs or work. Much of
Susan's life is modeled after the example of the Rev. Dr Martin Luther
King Jr. Although she never met the great civil rights leader and church-
man, he remains a significant figure in her life narrative.

I grew up in Indiana and was on my own in 1972. During that time
the KKK [Ku Klux Klan, a white supremacist group] still had a strong-
hold there. I had been involved in anti-war protests and I had a new
job. One night I was taking a stroll after work because I was trying to
unwind. I was walking down this dark street and I saw a shadow. At
first I was fearful and then I saw it was a human being. It was a young
black kid about my age. He had been sent to his relatives in this town,
but for some reason had run away. I grew up in a multicultural house.
I grew up in this mixed relationship and I had a flash of all of the
terrible possibilities that could happen. So I took this kid home and
gave him shelter. For six weeks he was with me. I met his family and
they said, 'Be careful.' About six weeks later he was putting his life
together and I looked out one day and the Klan was on my front lawn
burning a cross. It was sheer terror. I picked up the phone and called
the police and the operator said, 'Now honey, you want the sheriff.'
The next thing I knew, one of the Klansmen in my front yard had a
walkie-talkie and took his hood off and said, 'Do you want to talk to
me?' So they gave me their point of view and I gave them my point of
view. I called my dad. My dad cried and my mother said, 'How could
you do this to us?' My grandmother gave me a talk about being a
woman. The black boy's family came and told me how sorry they were.
I said, 'It's not your fault.' Then reporters showed up at my door. I did
some newspaper and TV and radio interviews. I told them that no
one, not even the Klan, would stop me from walking my path. So I
have been on the path ever since.

I am willing to help a total stranger. I am willing to be an advocate,
even when other people don't agree with me. I feel that's one of the
reasons why I am here in L'Arche. There will be conflicts in L'Arche,
but ultimately we have to support these people. It requires maturity

and compromise in order to embrace each other. I never looked back. I do not regret helping others.

*   *   *

Antonia is 25 years old. L'Arche caught hold of her shortly after college. She is the first of her family to have any post-secondary education, much less a degree. Antonia tells me that she 'bumped into' L'Arche after working with individuals with Down's syndrome at a nearby group home. Together, these residences would sometimes share activities in the community. Antonia is of medium height and overweight, with dark hair and a charismatic smile. Right now we are seated in the library of a L'Arche retreat center adjacent to her home.

> At the age of six my parents were big into drugs and at that age I had to become a mother to my little sister who was only four. I was really attached to her and I had an older sister who was ten and one day CPS [Child Protective Services] came in and they separated all three of us, and I was never separated from my family at all, had never been away from them. It is hard at the age of six when you have to take on the mother role. You have to worry about where your sister is and what she is doing.
>
> It all goes back to that helping thing; it is all about sticking your hand out and helping someone who is less fortunate than you. At that point in my life my little sister was dependent on me, and my older sister didn't know anything. She didn't know about cooking or anything about a house – I was the cook, I was the person who did the cleaning. It has been like a foundation for me; since about the age of ten I have been involved with the Salvation Army, so that is where it really started, where I began moving toward L'Arche and developing this idea that I need to help others. In the Salvation Army there was Delia, a black woman everyone called 'Mama Dee'. She took me under her wing and showed me how to love. [broadly smiling] When you have parents who are drug addicts you feel that you need to help others. You feel like you are a victim, but you also feel like you need to extend your hand. It has been a trying part but also feeling the need to help, the need to extend my hand. I have something that can help someone else. I couldn't live without knowing that I have something – a gift – and I am using it.

*   *   *

Chris is 33 years old, raffishly handsome with a prominent scar on his left temple. He is a long-term assistant in L'Arche. We are talking in the living room of his L'Arche home in the Pacific Northwest. Incessant rain is pouring from the sky. The prevailing gloom, however, is kept well outside this community. Candles are cheerfully burning in the living-room, smelling faintly of vanilla. Core members and assistants are enjoying a belly laugh in the kitchen. Chris is attentive throughout the interview, although I notice he often loses his train of thought.

I was driving a little Ford Escort – it happened in Vermont. I was driving on a country road, I don't remember the day – don't remember it at all. A Ford Explorer was coming. I was driving to a job interview. I was following directions on this sheet of paper and I made a wrong turn. Pulled over to the side of the road, went to do a U-turn and the Ford Explorer crashed into the driver's side door. It was a country road and it took them a long time to get me out. I was in the hospital for two and a half months. When I got out I went to the police department – what the hell happened? I was in a coma for two weeks, I was in the hospital for two and a half months. I remember when I was recovering I had different people helping out; vocational rehabilitation helped me to go back to work and I know how important that is. I know what that means not to be able to work and how important that is. So that is pretty much why I went into social work. I wanted to help people. After my accident, I realized there is more to the person than just the physical stuff. There is a lot more important stuff, you know. That is how I decided to go into social work. That is a lot of what L'Arche is about.

When I had my accident I was engaged and my fiancée stayed with me for a long time. She stayed with me for two years after the accident and helped me get on my feet. Then she left. She said that basically the doctors are right, you are not the same person any more. Two years after she left, I talked with her. I realized it wasn't that I had changed. It was that this person could not handle everything that we had gone through – she had her own problems and my situation was making things worse for her. I got a big part of myself back, then. In L'Arche hope is about much more than just me. Everyone has their own stuff. My own story reminds me that it is not all about me. In L'Arche you have to let the other stuff be. It is not connected to you. Be patient with people and hope for the best. In the meantime, I will help others just as I have been helped. My ex-fiancée helped me see it.

*   *   *

The legacy of helpers is clearly positive, even if the stories may end without everyone living happily ever after. Each assistant notes the influence of helpers at critical developmental crossroads in their experience. For Susan, it is the ideological weight of King's civil rights movement on her post-college notion of moral service. As a child in brutal circumstances, Antonia is befriended by Mama Dee at the Salvation Army. Chris is shaped by the care of his fiancée and trained medical professionals following a terrible accident. Helpers recognize aspects of human experience that are worth the high cost of compassionate love. Character grows as assistants learn to emulate helpers, aided by the hope that caring might become entrenched as an intergenerational legacy through the years. Hope illuminates the path which rivets Susan to a particular mission of advocacy. Hope frees Antonia from the trap of victimization. Hope grants Chris a matured capacity to focus on the other, recognizing that this is the most significant source of our identities.

It is worth noting that enemies are prominent in two of the narratives, particularly through Susan's account of the Ku Klux Klan. The terror enacted on the front lawn leads to an outcome completely opposite of Klan intentions. Galvanized by their actions, Susan is provoked into an even more radical position on civil rights than she might have been in the absence of intimidation. Hopeful character is deepened by the combined influences of helpers and enemies. Together, helpers and enemies are potent catalysts to assistant purpose. Each narrative yields wisdom through carefully wrought philosophies of human nature and experience. These philosophies are no accident. They trace their lineage to difficult circumstances which forced assistants to choose transcendent values of decidedly virtuous origin. Helpers and enemies provide real-world examples of these values and their potential consequences in human affairs.

Communion

The fourth theme identified in Walker's character project is *communion*. Morally mature individuals cherish platonic intimacy in relationships. In McAdams's view, this theme denotes strong commitment to the integrity of relationships. Communion places its hope in things like compassion, service, peace, and human interdependence. The theme is revealed through individual gifts as mediator and assistant. Communion happens with gentleness, warmth, and nurture. Communion may include a preference for intimacy through one-to-one relationship above group interac-

142

tions. Although women appear to be slightly more inclined toward communion in the research literature, men often understand themselves along these lines, particularly in places like L'Arche. It is important to consider the possibility that L'Arche not only fosters communion in core members and assistants, but may attract individuals who are predisposed to collective priorities. Communion might be understood as a signature theme for L'Arche, in large part because the philosophy of the charter so explicitly pulls for these character traits.

*   *   *

Lana is 53 years old – a firecracker personality not quite five feet tall. We are sitting on a sofa in the business office of a L'Arche network in the West. Lana is full of life and energy. She is a great friend of core members, assistants, and the mission of L'Arche. I am told by several others that Lana is the L'Arche 'mother' who first convinced them to become involved. Her enthusiasm is everywhere. As we talk, the business phone rings intrusively and the fax machine chatters periodically, causing me hidden annoyance. Lana is impervious. She merely becomes louder and more emphatic with her commentary.

Hope is being a birth partner for my niece. Also when I said 'Yes' to L'Arche. The flip side of this was when I was thinking of saying 'No' to L'Arche. I didn't think I could change my life. The importance of relationships . . . that is everything. Saying 'Yes' to L'Arche for me was letting go of the trappings I believed in when I was younger and still struggling with security. I don't need a lot in life, but I do need security. Saying 'Yes' to L'Arche put all of that security away. Retirement benefits, things like that. But what I said 'Yes' to is *life*. A quality of life where I live with people and have authentic relationships of love. That's what it was like watching my niece. Not just watching my sister give birth to her, but watching her develop and grow. That's life. It's an incredible experience. She's 16 now. I hate that she drives. [laughter] She accepts the fact that I'm a worrier. [chuckles] She rolls her eyes and puts up with me.

*   *   *

Erin is 34 and dressed in a retro skirt from the 1940s. Her hair is dyed black and bobbed, with a prominent blue streak. She is married to Phil,

143

another L'Arche assistant. Our conversation is privileged by a roaring fire, crackling and popping in the brick fireplace of her L'Arche home. We are sipping warm coffee as it is wet and cold outside. At first Erin is self-conscious about her narrative, periodically stopping and offering commentary about experiences and interpretations. This gradually disappears as she relaxes and settles in. A massive tabby cat jumps onto her lap and purrs loudly. Hope is a central theme in her story.

About a year and a half ago my dad had his stroke. I sat with my father and he was still pretty delusional. Strange, but I would say it was probably one of the greatest gifts I was ever given. At the time my dad was seeing things. He said to me, 'You have dirt all over your face, Erin, can you come over and sit by me?' So I came over and sat by my father and my dad took a cloth and for about ten minutes he wiped my face just like this [gesturing] and his hands were on my face. He kept wiping it and I gently sat there. It is probably the most amazing moment in my whole life – I knew I was beloved of God because I was beloved of my father, and I absolutely felt that. [long pause] So it was probably one of the greatest moments of my life. But it was something I would say I knew even more distinctly after the fact the more I prayed around it and knew it. So it was a pretty profound moment for me.

I was gone for a few weeks with my dad. When I came back, Phil told me that what happened with my dad was what he [Phil] had wished for months. Phil had been saying, 'I really hope that will come to you, that you know that you are beloved of God.' That is all of what L'Arche is to me, probably because I believe that my father's stroke caused him to become developmentally delayed. So it was hugely cyclical. My father's illness and death were absolutely intertwined with the L'Arche community. It was because of my father's death that I was able to accompany Robert [core member] in his death. Robert helped me accompany my dad in his death. It is all absolutely cyclical in that what we have lived allows us to live and fully celebrate relationships.

*   *   *

Dell is 29 years old, a tall African American from Georgia. He is a favorite with core members in this L'Arche community. On several occasions I observe Dell being hugged, kissed, or otherwise mobbed by the folk. Several of the core members refer to Dell by his nickname, 'Teddy'. The reference seems directed to the famous bear, although I am not certain. We are on the front porch of his L'Arche home on a street with enormous birch and maple trees. It's an unusually warm day in late fall. Children are at recess in a nearby elementary school. Dell is completing his third year in L'Arche.

I had a car accident a couple months ago which was completely my fault. Fortunately, nobody was injured. It was totally a misunderstanding with gravity and smashed up a couple of cars pretty bad. That was a couple months ago. It still has to get sorted out. My car was history. And then there was a legal application. It was a huge mess. It still is, but not as much. I have had a lot of epiphanies since then, about L'Arche, about life.

Well, when it happened, I couldn't have asked for better support. I was pretty shaken up, especially after that week. It could have been a lot worse. It really killed my confidence in myself. I was overwhelmed by the ramifications of it. A lot of people in L'Arche were praying for me. People who came by to make sure I was OK. I couldn't ask for more support. I felt like my family came through in a way. It taught me a lot about what community is about. You get caught up in all the daily conflicts and tensions . . . it is amazing when something really bad happens or someone dies how quickly we come together. It astounds me how we put a lot of things into perspective. It seems like we're so far away from everything which they say is living, but we come back to grace, what is important, to the priorities of why we are here.

L'Arche is a place for celebration. [smiling broadly] We love to celebrate. We celebrate birthdays and anniversaries. But that was not something that we did in my family when I was growing up. It took quite a few years for me to become comfortable with the idea. In the past I have tended to be quite introverted. In L'Arche there is quite a bit of extroverted energy. The last couple of birthdays where I was celebrated were very good for me. It gave me the opportunity to laugh and poke fun at myself and like myself and enjoy myself. But it also gave myself permission to say, 'Dell, you are a good person. People want to celebrate with you and you need to allow yourself to celebrate.' I didn't think I was good enough. Over time it has gotten better and the last couple of birthdays were a lot of fun for me, a lot of laughter and joking. A lot of silly things – games and skits. That was great because those are still major life events for me. Each time that we celebrate an anniversary it is further validation that I am a good person and that I am loved and people will allow themselves to love me. When it comes to celebrating it is a high point and I give myself permission and say, 'This is good – I can do this.' I don't burn energy thinking I don't deserve it. It is a lot easier now.

*   *   *

Communion is such a central fixture for L'Arche assistants that once identified, its presence becomes evident in nearly all the narratives recorded in this book. The above narratives offer a different spin on the communion theme as a dimension of life in L'Arche. In Lana's case, we sense that communion is nearly innate, a suite of traits that preceded her movement toward L'Arche but played an important role in solidifying her commitment. However, in Dell's narrative it appears that communion was desired, if elusive, before arriving in L'Arche. Time spent in the community raised the profile and importance of communion for Dell, leading to a new level of self-understanding. Communion may be built significantly on heartfelt wishes for intimacy. The development of communion is potentially furthered through spontaneous or unexpected events, such as Erin's extraordinary moment with her stroke-ravaged father.

The communion motif is powerfully associated with spiritual priorities. Erin's husband Phil makes religious interpretations of the encounter with her father as transcending time and space. While the specific details of assistant stories vary widely, the spiritual basis for communion is noteworthy across the majority of L'Arche assistant narratives. Elsewhere I have written that moral character is not reliant on religious or spiritual commitments, but often coincides with them.[9] One possible reason is that God becomes associated with hope and future-oriented possibility, at least in Western monotheism. Humans create narrative identities of enduring coherence where hope and awe are present reminders that moral commitments to real people (such as core members) celebrate compassionate possibilities that make the problems of our world bearable.

Hope, character, and compassionate goals

Hope nurtures character through the development of goals that allow L'Arche assistants to live consistently near their ideals. The four themes outlined above point to goals which become entrenched in assistant character through the practice of compassionate love. One aim for my L'Arche project was to study these goals as tangible outcomes of hope. The goals cherished by assistants in places like L'Arche tell us much about the nature of compassionate love. The development of goals happens in fits and starts, in large part through time spent with the core members of L'Arche. Accordingly, I asked caregiver assistants to write down 12–15 personal goals in order of greatest importance.[10] I separated assistant responses into two groups with the intention of considering developmental differences in character based on years served in L'Arche. The first group was known to have served for one year or less. The second group served for five or more years. Assistant goals were sorted with the use of a sophisticated computer program that mimics human learning.[11]

For newly arrived assistants, goals were organized into five clusters of meaning. The first cluster was termed *self-consistency* (e.g., 'ensure I am treated fairly', 'do my best', and 'do the right thing'). The second cluster was identified as *openness* (e.g., 'be open minded', 'make contact with others', and 'consider future directions'). The third cluster was named *adventure* (e.g., 'seek new experiences', 'be financially independent', and 'seek new relationships'). The fourth cluster was identified in terms of *empathy* (e.g., 'take care of people', and 'be helpful in stressful situations'). The fifth cluster was noted in terms of *lifestyle* (e.g., 'live simply', 'waste few resources', and 'eat less').

For long-term assistants, the first cluster was named *balance* (e.g., 'find balance between work, prayer, and play', and 'practice patience'). The second cluster was understood in terms of *groundedness* (e.g., 'make time to garden', 'keep in touch with friends', and 'find space to relax'). The third cluster was framed in terms of *self-care* (e.g., 'take a nap', 'go for walks', and 'sit calmly for 20 minutes'). The fourth cluster was identified as *interpersonal responsibility* (e.g., 'forgive others who hurt me', 'maintain good relationship with my staff', and 'give love to those I serve'). The fifth cluster was named *awe and ethics* (e.g., 'look at stars', 'live in gratitude', and 'be a godly disciple').

To my thinking, the goal classification process made good sense in outlining a better understanding of behaviors that arise with the development of character. Newly arrived L'Arche assistants mention goals related to identity formation. In effect, rookie assistants are attempting to find themselves while mapping the priorities of the community. They must quickly and correctly read the intentions of others – a daunting task when working with developmentally disabled persons who may lack the ability to communicate clearly. In particular, *empathy* suggests a capacity to understand the perspectives and feelings of other people, helping cultivate an interpersonal ethic given to care. For this assistant group, goals are highly social. Consistent with their status as newly arrived participants in a community, goals are geared toward improving self-understanding across a range of diverse relationships. Assistants are preoccupied with getting along with others and figuring things out. Central to their goals is a spirituality of action before contemplation, seasoned with a measure of idealism.

By contrast, long-term assistants offer more contemplative goal systems, demonstrating a marked capacity for self-reflection. Idealism is tempered by recognition of personal limitation and the means by which spiritual insights emerge through difficult circumstances. These are the mature goals of people with clearly defined boundaries relative to community. While L'Arche values are abundantly evident in the narratives of long-term assistants, there is evidence of creative synthesis and revision. The L'Arche emphasis on simple living is reframed around *self-care* such as taking a nap. Spiritual commitments are sprinkled throughout the clusters, some carrying moral implications. Long-term assistants are looking for concrete ways of integrating spirituality into the most mundane aspects of daily life. Responsibility, fidelity, love, and fairness are hallmark character standards – virtues by which these assistants attempt to live. The path is characterized by weathered morality and spirituality. Hope reminds L'Arche members that the highest ideals of community are realized in earthy and sometimes painful circumstances.

Road to Guadalupe

I am enjoying the party immensely. Sayid's double cheeseburgers are restaurant worthy, although we are afterward troubled with thoughts about artery disease. The water balloon war is a tremendous success – Katarina blissfully hurls multicolored grenades in every direction. Wet hair is plastered to her face. Her chuckles are music as she catches spray from returned fire. Half of the group is soaked from head to toe. The rest exist in varied states of dampness. Many are giggling uncontrollably. The sun is now completely beneath the horizon and the night is warm. I can hear cicadas singing chorus scales. With masterful timing, Cherise emerges from the back door with an enormous chocolate cake peppered with glowing candles. The water balloon war is forgotten as the group encircles Cherise, who has grabbed Katarina and pulled her into the center of the circle next to the cake. The group is suddenly quiet.

While the candles slowly burn, people offer spontaneous blessings and words of thanks for Katarina. Core members and assistants together praise a disabled woman encumbered with profound difficulties. It is an arresting demonstration of sincere, unfiltered compassionate love. The birthday party is a celebration of hope, recognizing that our path is one of growth reflecting character. The path is open to anyone willing to acknowledge before self, others, and God that we are all disabled, yet nonetheless respected. As we sit with plates of cake, I again find myself next to Nancy. She shares an epilogue.

I went on a pilgrimage to Our Lady of Guadalupe in Mexico. We went with L'Arche members [both core members and assistants] from two different communities. Supposedly we were going to beg for food and lodging. That attracted me. I let my leader know that I was going. Just the experience of being free enough to do that was an important part of the experience and the other part was being with this group. We were supposed to sleep with migrant farm workers, but it didn't work out. We had to find lodging unexpectedly. People were saying to me, 'You are the one who wants to beg, so beg!' I saw a school with the lights on. We went over and knocked on the door. People answered and I told them who we were and asked them if it was possible for us to sleep on the gym floor. It was the janitor and he showed us to the principal. We told the principal that we were on a pilgrimage and we had disabled people with us.

The janitor looked at the principal and said, 'How can we not offer them shelter?' So they let us spend the night. They called the entire faculty who came and made breakfast for us. They signed our petition for Our Lady of Guadalupe. They gave us money for gas. All of this happened because we simply asked to be housed. For me that was the opening of someone else's heart to see the call. It was an incredible experience. We took that with us the whole time. It's a good thing, too! We thought the train went all the way to Guadalupe. But it didn't. We got off the train and had to bus it. There were five of us who wanted to walk the last 15 miles into the city of Guadalupe. By accident, the bus driver let us off 25 miles from town. We had only one poncho and blanket and we were freezing. The bus driver told us that if we needed help, to hail another bus. One person in our group had terrible blisters on her feet and we hailed many buses but no one stopped.

We walked and walked but we did not talk. Sometimes I prayed the rosary – this was a prayerful journey. When we finally got into Guadalupe it was a wonderful feeling; we've made it! We were staying in a convent there. It was all part of the experience. We spent some time with the people. Even though I didn't know Spanish there was great communication. We went back to the convent and asked if we could bring people from the barrio with us. They wouldn't – they were adamant. So six of us said we won't stay here either. We got some bread and cheese and wine and went to the barrio and shared it with the poor. Those three things were all a part of the same experience. When you talk about the call and compassion and the gospel you talk about L'Arche as a way of entering into people's lives. That was all a part of that journey. It wasn't the way it was planned to be. There was so much in the journey that you could never have planned – the kind of spontaneous trust that you take one step at a time. It certainly taught me that it's OK to have that spontaneity. Instead of planning and saying what are we going to do, you just say, 'We're going to do this.' It's that whole sense of spontaneous hope, that sense of service. It's not what you give, it's what you are. How you are. To never lock the doors if someone comes knocking.

7

The Fragile Ark

The idea of the service of humanity, of brotherly love and the solidarity of mankind, is more and more dying out in the world, and indeed this idea is sometimes treated with derision.

(*Fyodor Dostoevsky*)[1]

It is turbulent over the Atlantic. The massive jetliner shakes and leaps with surprising agility through the difficult air. The captain explains that we are navigating the edge of a powerful storm. Eastbound flights typically benefit from favorable tailwinds. Not tonight. Dinner service is canceled with passengers tersely instructed to fasten belts. Anxiety festers throughout the flexing cabin. Rattles and thumps become louder with increasingly violent movement. Flight attendants are closely strapped into five-point jump seats like astronauts preparing for launch. Grasping for normalcy, complete strangers begin talking with one another. It turns out that my seatmate is involved in the trade of fine wines. He regularly travels to the world's famed wine-growing regions. Fresh from a tour of the Maipo Valley in Chile, he is heading to Bordeaux on this Paris-bound flight. Conversation turns to my work. I avoid tiresome detail, focusing on broad topics of research interest. He is intrigued with the notion of moral psychology. Enthusiasm evaporates, however, with the mention of compassionate love and L'Arche. The plane drops heavily into an air pocket, momentarily taking our breath. Regaining attitude, his response becomes an acerbic terminus to the exchange. 'My sister does social work. She was a hippie in college – a dreamer. All those good vibrations are fine in the commune, but don't amount to much on Main Street.'

Some hours later I am visiting with eight disabled core members in a small living-room.[2] The country home is located in a northern French village named Trosly-Breuil. Prevailing chatter and laughter make his entrance anonymous, nearly unnoticed. The elderly gentleman is very tall and slightly stooped, with snowy hair which years ago might have been chocolate. His eyes are shaded with compassion. Like a priest he moves deliberately about the room touching core members with familiar grace. His hands shake slightly. While he speaks little, he knows each individual by name. Exchanges are brief but intense – core members manifest welcome with effusive warmth. A bearded assistant named Bernard enters from the kitchen, ushering the group to the lunch table. The meal is simple and typically L'Arche: mushroom quiche served on paper plates. The older man sits at my left, leading the group in a prayer of thanksgiving. Our conversation is interrupted by spontaneous interactions with core members and assistants. He politely asks about my journey to France. I mention the rough ride and sardonic seatmate. An enormous smile creases the worn face. Eyes twinkle impishly. Nodding vigorously, Jean Vanier repeats an observation echoed through the research study: 'L'Arche is impossible.'

L'Arche is a cultural eccentric, buffeted by swirling currents of cynicism, social misperception, and everyday needs. It is a gossamer vessel of compassionate and loving intentions. My purpose in this final chapter is to consider the ever-widening paradox of L'Arche through insights of individuals who regularly transcend the improbable. The difficulties confronting L'Arche are daunting. Financial and personnel concerns simmer throughout the American L'Arche zone. Assistants reflect on these and other problems through the refinery of personal experience. Following the format of Chapter 1, assistant reflections are suffixed with core member observations. The chapter additionally includes narrative from an informal conversation with caregiver assistants over lessons learned from years of living compassionately and lovingly. The chapter concludes with a final narrative underscoring L'Arche identity as beloved – a sign for a decadent and impersonal Western culture. There are no banner prescriptions or demands attached. With humblest intentions, L'Arche ratifies human dignity through compassionate and loving prerogatives.

Cold coffee

Hot coffee is rapidly cooling. Conversation in this urban bistro swiftly unfolds without caffeine. My dialogue partner is a human dynamo by the name of Sophia Schmidt. She is zone coordinator of L'Arche USA. The meeting agenda is the research project and findings, but things quickly evolve into a discussion of hurdles which face the movement in its American context. Her face is expressive through the narrative.

This is the most challenging thing I've ever done. Many of our communities are financially on thin ice. Local directors always have to deal with the reality of budget needs. Some of it ends up in my lap. I was recently on a trip to one of our communities. They've been fortunate for the past few years. The state government picked up about half of their operating expenses. But now the state budget is on the rocks. Social services took a big hit and the local director was really stressed out. She was looking at ways to come up with the shortfall. All the while money was becoming tighter and tighter. They had cash for food but things were touch-and-go over regular bills like electricity and heat. So we mapped out a game plan which included city government and other private sources. Grants and the like.

We got through that pickle, but it wasn't much fun. My director friend couldn't sleep for a few months. I realize that people in the corporate world have their ups and downs too. But the stakes feel higher for us. Vulnerable people rely on us. They know when things aren't looking good. It's not easy fielding questions from core members who know something's wrong. We want them to feel secure, to know things aren't going to fall apart. My brother's a corporate accountant and he doesn't have to face core members and assistants at community gatherings or meals. The issues are different for him. I suppose everyone's faith is growing in the midst of these struggles. But it isn't much fun at the time.

The financial issues don't end there. I'm sure you've noticed that many of our homes are old. Some are from the Victorian era – more than a century old. There's lots of upkeep involved with these places, not to mention the fact that when things break they can be expensive to fix. One of our homes in the East required a new roof to the tune of $22,000. The board and I have been on a mission lately. We've started a capital campaign to help address some of the problems. Everything from new roofs to remodeled space to property. We've had to become good at presentations and grant solicitations. We have a great board of directors. They are passionate for L'Arche. Many are networked into financial and service industries. Some have background in development and fundraising. I feel really blessed that they've given us such support and vision for our capital campaign.

What are your growing edges for the future?

Finances aren't the full extent of our challenges. Probably the single biggest concern I have about L'Arche is recruitment and retention of caregiver assistants. Your study is a help to us in this regard. We'll find out what they're thinking in a slightly different way. We have discernment and lots of regular communication to keep assistants from becoming isolated. To make sure they get the care and support they need. We know they need a lot of this. L'Arche can be really difficult. We have a problem with assistant burnout and turnover. It varies from community to community, but we sometimes lose a lot of our new assistants within a year of welcome. We also experience turnover among our long-term assistants.

There are aspects of burnout and turnover beyond our control. Some assistants come to L'Arche with wounds that are so huge they can't function well. Or the community can't effectively hold their suffering. It wouldn't matter if they were in L'Arche or working in any other field. They'd probably have a difficult time making it through. But there's another group where we can make a difference. These assistants start well, but become tired and sometimes depressed over the months. We badly want to find new ways to support and nurture these assistants. It's more than a compensation thing – they don't tell us they're leaving because of money. The problems are deeper; more related to things like interpersonal conflicts and misunderstanding. Stress. We are looking for ways to better enfold new assistants into the community. It's another aspect of welcome, but one with significant consequences in terms of our vitality. When an assistant leaves prematurely, it is terribly difficult for core members. They make a bond and then 'poof!' the person is gone.

We are pretty different, yes. L'Arche is unlike anything else. [brightening] There's great beauty in difference. I think we can offer the world a different understanding of disability, or the matter of compassionate love which you are studying. Certainly we can show the world a different view of what it means to be human. Many of us believe that L'Arche is the sign of a different way, a life of downward mobility and Christian spirituality. The ideas behind L'Arche are big ideas. We are a big idea kind of movement. This can cause misunderstanding or cynicism. People don't know what to do with us. They might even feel a little threatened. But we can't lose sight of the core members and assistants. Regardless of how outsized we think our ideas might be, we still have basic needs. Financial needs or personnel needs. We still need to put food on the table.

The conversation ends abruptly with the realization that everything on the table is cold. Sophia is slightly embarrassed at her impassioned diatribe, but I am grateful for the candor. Her perspective is wide and her view is long. Sophia is a visionary who successfully balances the big picture with practical realism from years of experience as a caregiver assistant. Her observations begin on the ground in L'Arche. More than likely, the twin challenges of finances and personnel are aggregations of many smaller concerns which together fuel larger conflagrations.

Down in the trough

Compassionate love is work. It is what comes after warm sensations are gone. It is commitment to relationship in the wake of joy, excitement, or celebration. The compassionate love of L'Arche flourishes where Katarina is loved through a tantrum shortly after her birthday party. It deepens where Dell is supported through his car accident and subsequent weeks of litigation. It persists through the clean-up of Nellie's living-room vomit. Successful resolution of financial and personnel concerns in L'Arche requires that members learn compassionate love as *discipline*. This is a difficult pill; an affront for persons reared in an instant society. The grittier terms of compassion are unexpected, distasteful, or potentially ludicrous. Persons socialized by Western notions of success and prosperity may find little immediate reward for their commitment. There is no overtime pay in L'Arche. Relatives may misinterpret assistant motives for service. Expectations for advancement must be reshuffled following exposure to downwardly mobile values. Community discernment focuses on personal growth and spiritual direction rather than prestige. Compassionate love invites risk and discomfort through ever-possible rejection.

Member insight regarding compassionate commitment often coincides with moments of stress or trouble, a porthole into underlying problems which contribute to Sophia's concerns for financial stability and personnel retention. L'Arche members often mentioned experiences where they came to understand compassionate love as demanding and fragile. These were typically revealed through observation or informal exchanges outside the interview setting. I have recorded several such vignettes below. Each offers perspective on compassionate love as discipline in community. All recognize that love matters greatly and costs more than anyone dared to anticipate. The vignettes reveal a heavily trafficked intersection between big ideas and real-world struggle.

*   *   *

Alan is 28 years old and exhausted. A caregiver assistant, he joins me in the living room of his L'Arche home in the Eastern United States. For the past 90 minutes Alan worked through a bipolar episode with a core member upstairs. Screams and loud crashes were audible through the floor. The core member is finally in bed. Flushed and slightly out of breath, Alan sits facing the television which is tuned to the History Channel. The program details the Battle of Midway, a crossroads in the conflict between the American and Japanese navies during the Second World War. Nationalistic bias unapologetically suffuses the presentation. However, the black-and-white film footage is interesting. I am fascinated by a clip showing large warships cresting enormous waves in the open Pacific. Alan is similarly intrigued.

I'm from the Chesapeake Bay region of Maryland. I love the ocean. My dad owned a 26-foot sailboat which we took out all the time. We'd sail that little sloop from one end of the bay to the other. The Chesapeake is pretty unpredictable. It can be windy or calm or sometimes really stormy. I think my sailing experience taught me a lot about what to expect from L'Arche. There was one day we were involved in a race to a marker outside the bay, in the open ocean. The conditions were pretty marginal – lots of wind and some chop left over from a nor'easter. Once we turned into the open ocean it got much worse. I'd never sailed in conditions like that before. The swell grew to more than 12 feet and the wind was steady at over 30 miles per hour. We soon realized we were in over our heads and turned around for home. Many others in the fleet did the same.

The scariest part of that day was being down in the trough between swells. You can't let the boat get turned sideways in the trough, or the waves can roll you right over. When you're down in the trough you're thinking about it constantly. You're not thinking about anything else. Along with a tight grip on the tiller, you have to keep your head and keep the faith. You have to realize you're going to come up over the top to see where you're headed. You can make course corrections at the top of the wave. But down in the trough it's all about keeping the boat from turning sideways. If that happens, it's curtains for everyone. The water is cold in the Atlantic. We knew that if our boat rolled, we wouldn't survive long in the cold water. L'Arche is like our sailboat. You don't realize how big the seas can get. In the beginning you don't understand how much commitment it takes to stay with the core members and other assistants. You learn in a hurry, or you roll over into the sea.

It is breakfast the next morning. The bipolar core member continues to struggle. The table scene begins normally, with members passing cereal boxes, milk, or plates of toast. Somehow our bipolar friend feels slighted. The specific offense isn't obvious to the rest of us, but this makes little difference. Alan and another assistant reassure the core member that no malfeasance was intended. Both work closely together, complementing the other's moves. Their patience is inspiring. Nevertheless, food and cutlery fly after a vitriolic outburst from the core member. The group takes a collective breath, as if people are retrenching themselves around the common goal of remaining together and upright through the turmoil. A core member stoops to the floor and picks up fallen cutlery. An assistant gets a broom and dustbin for dispersed cereal. Actions unfold without shame or condemnation. Alan continues to talk with the bipolar individual. Progress becomes evident. The core member visibly relaxes. Breakfast conversation resumes, albeit at muted volume. Despite forward movement, residual stress persists. The laughter and bantering native to this community are temporarily vanished.

*   *   *

Collette is 24 years old, an assistant for 12 months in this L'Arche community. We are at the holiday beach described in Chapter 1. I am sitting in a folding chair, avoiding sunburn by adjusting to the shadow of a blue parasol stuck firmly into the sand. Collette is reading a novel, *The Brothers Karamazov*. Bored, she puts down the book and begins a conversation. We talk about past community holidays and activities. The group continues to endure a measure of transition and upheaval with Robert's passing, the addition of new core members, and the departure of assistants. Collette seems philosophical about the changes until the conversation takes an unexpectedly personal turn.

> You want to know the real story? The core members aren't the only ones who hurt when people leave the community. There was an assistant who left suddenly and I had a lot of hope about that relationship. There are so few people here who are my age. He was 23 and we had a lot of stuff in common and I was really hoping that there would be something romantic between us. One day he up and left. Well, not quite. He actually gave two days' notice. But he took off on a plane and left. Just like that. In L'Arche we talk about saying 'Yes' to something and here he was saying 'No' to me and saying 'No' to our lives in

community as a whole. It was depressing. I'm still a bit down about it. How could this happen? He was fantastic with the core members. Sometimes we let good people slip through our fingers. He was not even here for two months. I am sorry that things like this happen and that they are allowed to happen in the first place. That someone wasn't comfortable with the structure. Or didn't feel secure enough to share when he was struggling. That he wasn't able to admit to himself that he was struggling. That he didn't feel this was going to work for him. I've never felt trapped here and I've always felt like this was my decision. His leaving made me strive to be more open about when I am struggling. To seek out other people when I am having problems. Even more important, to reach out to others more intentionally. Not to let people fall through the cracks.

Collette pulls out a deck of cards. We extend an open invitation for a game of poker. Half a dozen people are soon in the circle. Avram is a young core member with good verbal skills. Even before the first hand, it's evident that Avram struggles with the basic concept of the game, but desperately wants to fit in. He feigns experience with poker, telling stories about his late-night gambling exploits in a manner reminiscent of last night's movie thriller. It's a delicate business affirming Avram while sustaining the game. In a striking demonstration of collective adaptation, the group attempts to learn Avram's 'rules' on the sly, as he works through the hand. Almost as fast as the 'rules' are learned, assistants verbally 'remind' the group how the game is played. Soon we are playing a card game which only distantly resembles poker. But some insist that this is the real deal – authentic Texas hold 'em, just like the early frontier cattle drives. Afterward I am mildly troubled, wondering if our efforts were too deceptive. Without question the goal of affirming Avram is significant. But are group charades the way to do it? As if reading my mind, Collette looks over and shrugs. 'There's no use worrying if it was right or wrong. We do our best with what we have; let the chips fall where they may.'

*　　　*　　　*

Laurie is 27 years old, a first-year caregiver assistant. A native of Houston, her family is originally from Venezuela. I'm finishing my second week in this Midwestern L'Arche community. I've offered to cook everyone dinner as a gesture of thanks. Laurie is sous chef, cheerily mincing vegetables and readying cooking utensils. By community request I am making a boutique meal. The menu is linguine with white clam sauce, steamed broccoli and shaved Asiago cheese, grilled sourdough garlic bread, Waldorf salad, and tiramisu for dessert. I'm preoccupied with getting quantities right for 17 people. Laurie is happily oblivious, cleanly dicing shallots with a medium-sized cleaver. She is talkative and articulate.

You often don't realize how paper-thin things are in L'Arche. I got my driver's license a few months ago for the first time. If you can believe it, I spent nine months in L'Arche without a driver's license. Just reaching the point of getting it was huge. I feel so much more competent now because I can do the doctor's appointments. I can do things from start to finish instead of working in the office or handing things off to other people. Two days after I got my driver's license we had this huge crisis and I was the only assistant in the house. Tiffany [core member] had climbed over the baby gate. She's not supposed to have access to the kitchen because she likes to play with knives. [shakes head] Not very safe! No one knows how it happened, but somehow she fell and impaled her leg on the gate. So there was one spike of the gate in her leg. I heard her fall but there was no blood at all. The wound was just huge. It took three EMTs [emergency medical technicians] to get the gate out of her leg and it was just a huge bloody mess, basically. But I had my driver's license and was able to follow the ambulance to the hospital and take care of things for her. A driver's license can make a big difference when a crisis hits.

Things can turn south in a real hurry around here. At the time of Tiffany's accident I was the only assistant in the house for two weeks. I had to ask for a lot of support. Eventually I got it. It was really stressful knowing that I'm the only one in charge. I'm the one running things and telling people what I need them to do. The leadership was great. Maggie [local director] had full faith in me. She knew my personality and was confident, even though she's detail oriented and I'm not. So it was a stretch to think that this is what needs to be done and I need to ask you to do it. Of course, it's an even bigger stretch when one of the core members impales her leg on the baby gate. I grew a lot through that experience, although in the moment I wondered if I was out of my mind for being here.

Dinner is a complete success. Core members and assistants feel appreciated and slightly stuffed. The group disperses slowly. Core members and assistants from other residences walk home in the night. Our house is left with four core members and two assistants, including Laurie. The home is short-staffed with the recent departure of Manny, an assistant who left for the Philippines after six weeks of service. Two of the core members are non-verbal. One of these individuals has mobility problems, requiring a considerable amount of direct assistance. Laurie and her partner scurry about the house getting everyone ready for bed. Independently they offer apologies for leaving me with the gourmet aftermath in dining room and kitchen. Cleanup takes a solid hour of steady work. At long last I sit down in the living room. For yet another hour I am alone. The wall clock strikes 10 p.m. Finally, two weary assistants come down the stairs. Both offer thanks for the clean kitchen. But instead of a good book or other means to unwind, each moves on to a new chore. Laurie settles in the office to complete paperwork. Her partner resumes work on the laundry, folding small items from a waist-high pile of clothes. She smiles wanly, deep circles beneath her eyes, 'I swear the laundry is breeding. It never ends!'

*   *   *

Kelly is 54 years old, a long-term assistant with tenure across multiple L'Arche communities in different states. At her invitation, we are working together on the front garden of her L'Arche residence. She moves slowly, the result of arthritis and multiple knee surgeries. Kelly loves the garden, but seems resigned to the growing likelihood that her active days are numbered. Right now, we are tending mammoth rose bushes on the property line. Cream, red, and pink roses create a fragrant privacy wall between houses. Kelly trims branches with shears, leaving me to pick out remains for the wheelbarrow. The summer day is warm and bees are humming nearby.

> Now that I'm getting older, I'm forced to face my physical problems in a different way. It's tough because I don't have medical insurance here, although my husband has very basic coverage through his job in town. Our deductible is high, which means I'm gritting it out. It's nothing new. For years I've had trouble because of problems with my knees, and finding out other kinds of physical anomalies, abnormalities that I have. You know, finding out that I need surgeries. I have this thing about making it ten years between each surgery and I didn't make it ten years between the last one for my left knee and the one for my right knee. I had three surgeries in three years after college. I had this doctor who, after the first surgery didn't work, told me it was all

in my head. Can you believe it? Friends weren't real understanding, so I had a lot of issues around not being able to do things and I would push myself to do things that I maybe shouldn't do, like climbing a mountain. I'm slowly coming to the realization that there are things that I won't be able to do. It's hard, because L'Arche is that mountain for me. You've got to have mobility to work with the core members.

I'm looking at total knee replacement surgeries. I'd like to put it off until I'm 60; you know, that ten-year thing. But I don't know if I'll be able to continue here, even with the surgery. I knew when I had surgery on my right knee that I will eventually have to have both of my knees replaced. Many of the core members have physical problems too. We do our best, but sometimes life deals you a tough hand. It is hard to accept that there are things that I just can't do, especially when I see a lot of other people doing things that I really want to be able to do and I know I just can't. Or I will try to do things that I know I shouldn't and end up paying the price. It makes me realize how disabled we are, all of us.

When I had my first surgery and didn't get better, my friends weren't very understanding. It was, 'Well, you'll have surgery and you'll get better.' [pauses to untangle rose branches from clothing] I didn't get well and there wasn't a lot of support there, so I learned to avoid talking about how I was feeling. That was a defense mechanism that I developed pretty early on, and it is one that is still in place. It is one that I have a hard time getting over and I know it's there, and I try and try, kind of like climbing a 20-foot wall. I am not as open as I would like to be and I am not as trusting as I would like to be. I tend to feel easily betrayed, so I don't put a lot out there that people can betray. I think that is probably one of the biggest challenges in L'Arche, to get over that. L'Arche really challenges me, because I am being forced to face it a lot. I know it is not easy, but I am choosing to work on that particular thing, to grow through it.

Today is Tuesday – shopping day. Kelly moves through the kitchen with notepad and pen, listing items in short supply. She has already visited the garage pantry and basement storage, taking stock of paper products and canned goods. It is Kelly's habit to visit the supermarket with Walter, an elderly core member. Walter greatly enjoys the outing which often includes a pause for donuts and coffee. The good man is following Kelly around the kitchen with anticipation. Finally the inventory is complete. Kelly grabs handbag and keys, heading out the front door to the community van parked on the street. Seconds after the front door closes, I hear a dull thud which rattles the downstairs windows. Concerned, I get up to investigate. Looking through the front window, I can see the stooped figure of Walter, arm clasped tightly around Kelly's shoulders. Apparently she fell on the front steps. The culprit is her right knee which she favors, leaning into Walter for support. The two slowly make their way to the van, looking like trainer and veteran athlete headed toward the bench after collision with an opposing player. Kelly's expression is fixed and almost blank; the look of chronic pain. Suddenly Walter looks back at the house. Making eye contact, he nods quickly in my direction, as if to say, 'She'll be all right.'

*   *   *

I am with Adam, a young caregiver assistant introduced in Chapter 2. We are taking core member Danny to the doctor's office. The staff whisk Danny away for his blood pressure check. In the waiting room we randomly leaf through magazines and medical pamphlets. A three-year-old boy methodically tours the room, catching and rewarding our attention with a dazzling smile. Adam reads a *National Geographic* issue which includes a special feature on Ireland. The pictures are emerald portraits of windswept County Donegal and its hardy inhabitants. He looks up from the magazine with a thoughtful stare.

The article makes me think of three months I recently had with L'Arche in Ireland. It was quite a study in contrasts. Our L'Arche community is pretty solid in terms of finances – probably much better off even than others in the American zone. But things were completely different for L'Arche over there. They have enough money for the house and food, but it is really tight. It is nothing like it is here. The interesting thing is, you'd never know. They still have a good time. They can't go out to the movies or dinner in order to have fun. Instead, they go to the park – have a picnic and things like that. It really shakes you up; realizing how much unnecessary consumption happens here. Coming back across the pond I see things differently. I see how much people have that they really don't need in order to be happy. There is not a lot of money to be made doing this kind of work. I keep reminding myself of the studies I heard about in college; there is no correlation between how much money you make and how happy you are. I understood that more clearly coming from Ireland,

162

which of course is nothing like L'Arche in India or Haiti. The experience really changed how I view things here. I am not going to come back and preach that to people. If you don't live it first, it is hard to understand. But it definitely changed the way I see things.

Still, you can't go home again. Literally! [chuckling] It is much harder now, where in the summer we can afford to go out to music festivals or take the core members into town. It is tough because three out of the four core members in our house, they like to shop; that is what they like to do more than anything else. They go out and buy things. Not to use stuff, but just to have it in possession. They really like to shop. I struggle a lot with it. I've suggested we try to do more simple things, stuff that doesn't require a lot of money or that's fun for simple reasons. My trip to Ireland is carrying over into how I live. I hope it's not a put-off for anyone. I really don't mean to judge. But we need to be good stewards of what we've been given.

On the way back from the doctor's office we stop downtown. Like many American cities, local government is investing large sums of money toward rehabilitation of urban neighborhoods. Restorative construction is everywhere. Our errand involves filling a prescription for Danny. Parking is tight. We are forced to park two blocks from the pharmacy. On the way, we encounter a balding homeless gentleman with a grizzled white beard. He sits next to a shopping cart filled with sleeping bag, tarp, and aluminium cans. Danny stops abruptly. Realizing he carries no cash, Danny looks to us entreatingly on behalf of the homeless man. Adam and I each reach into our pockets and discover we're no better off. What to do? Adam finds the solution. Spotting a nearby sandwich shop, we offer to buy the homeless gentleman a meal using credit. Danny is delighted. He asks the man for an order, which turns out to be tremendously detailed. I am dumbfounded to hear Danny painstakingly relay each request to the sandwich maker in perfect sequence. The homeless man solemnly takes his sandwich and turns to leave without a word. Back on the street Danny begins to skip, lightly moving on toes which pointedly and skillfully avoid pavement cracks.

*   *   *

Doug is a long-term assistant introduced in Chapter 3. Along with a colleague, Doug is leading seven core members home after Mass. The wind is blowing strongly on this Sunday morning. Clouds and storm scud rapidly overhead at low altitude. Trees bend before the gusts with leaves flying horizontally like wisps of a child's dandelion. Chilled, we walk quickly to stay warm. Everyone is muffled against the cold. Doug and I are at the front of the group. Our conversation is mostly about the homily. The message considered the importance of obedience in faith. Elements of the Old Testament reading strike a deeper chord for Doug.

This is a tough time I've been going through, mostly over the question of God's hand in community. Somewhere in scripture it says that although he shall kill me I will still trust in him. I feel very deeply a crushing hand over the past ten months. I also see Jesus throughout the whole thing, I really do. I see him calling me to take part in his passion. In his redemptive ministry. I believe that's one of the greatest dignities bestowed upon us, to take part in God's redemptive ministry. Serving our neighbors, helping in salvation. Suffering is redemptive as we see on the cross. That's God's ace in the hole. His wild card that he played in the end. Death was death and now it is life. I've felt that, and it has been such a painful experience, but I can see the other end and these people in community are instruments of God. I can see this in terms of a call to community, to greater growth, a call to greater love. Greater sacrificial love. I see a significant event in the community in terms of where I've revealed things about myself. I've had a safe place to do that. An oasis of trust where I can reveal parts of myself that I wouldn't normally share. Feeling safe in that. The environment of sacredness, where our paths and stories are respected. Being valued and respected and taken care of.

Probably because of the difficulties, my whole dynamic has changed. Inside L'Arche I notice selflessness in other people much more. I think this is what I struggle with the most. When I walk into these situations I still think about myself first. Redemptive ministry isn't easy. Becoming a leader in our community, I began to understand why I have to think of the other person first. In L'Arche, that is what it is all about. I am learning every day how to think about someone else before I think about myself. This is sort of a double-edged sword, actually. It opened my eyes to the importance of growth. One of the most challenging aspects of following Jesus is trying to remove all those walls that have been built up over the years. It's like realizing you've been racist and then trying to break it down. To take those stereotypes down, take the wall out of your head, and just accept people for what they are.

We reach the house. Exposed body parts are numbed by the cold. My nose feels artificial, like a prosthetic appendage. The great wind assails windows and eaves with a deep-throated howl. Inside, core member Thomas tunes the television to a professional football game. Doug walks into the kitchen and listens to voicemail. Several minutes later he emerges. His eyes smolder darkly with frustration. Two other assistants join him in the kitchen. They converse in muted tones for a tense hour. An assistant named Harriet eventually comes out, informing the football audience that we are going for pizza. It becomes clear that Doug will not be joining us. As Harriet drives, she explains the situation in a low voice. Doug, who is house responsible, was told last week that the understaffed home will shortly welcome two caregiver assistants. For different reasons, both have fallen through. Harriet tells me that Doug is an exceptional leader who feels the burden of his colleagues and wants badly to alleviate their stress. At the pizzeria, core members are enjoying dinner. Several use quarters to play video games. One game is a smash favorite, seating players inside a mock Formula I car racing through the streets of Los Angeles. Harriet pulls together leftovers while I find a box. She wraps several pieces of pepperoni pizza in a napkin emblazoned with the name 'Doug'. Carefully separating these from other pieces, she looks up at me. 'Doug lives for pepperoni.'

*   *   *

Compassionate love persists through everyday tumult and ongoing stressors. Discipline isn't learned overnight. The vignettes suggest that core members and assistants have spent weeks, months, and years learning to overcome obstacles in compassionate practice. Alan's depiction of the deep hollow between dangerous waves confers skillful perseverance in provision of care. The discipline of love is acquired through repeated risk to self through rejection. Compassionate lovers may get wet or, worse, end up swimming in rough seas without immediate rescue. We have no idea whether the bipolar core member will respond to Alan's compassionate initiative. It is unclear if the homeless man will accept Danny's sandwich. Getting up after an embarrassing and painful fall, Kelly must decide to share Walter's quiet strength. In each instance, compassionate love finds its target. But there is no guarantee of future returns. L'Arche members are often fatigued. The laundry is breeding. People stumble and fall badly. New assistants change plans and leave others dangling without support.

The vignettes yield three features of compassionate discipline which subsequently illuminate the financial and personnel concerns shared over cooling coffee. First, core members and assistants must realign *expectations* of community life based on immediate realities. Collette's frank admission of romantic interest in a male assistant tempers expectations for relationship with the fickle transience of human commitment. Her pain surfaces through acknowledgement that the relationship will not materialize. It is imperative that she find other reasons to stick with the community. Her love finds purpose through the inclusion of those who otherwise might be unwelcome. Adam discovers that the simplicity of downward mobility is shaded by different economic and cultural influences. Downward mobility may be a quintessential L'Arche hallmark, but it varies greatly depending on context. The simple life differs in Haiti relative to Ireland compared with the United States. To avoid cynicism and gentrification, Adam looks for creative ways to live downward mobility in a manner which keeps compassion supple and love engaged. Whatever expectations these and other individuals brought with them to L'Arche, the situation on the ground requires adaptation and creativity. The story of compassionate love for each author is a dynamic tale, never completely written or definitively resolved.

Second, compassionate L'Arche members at times *resign* themselves to the physical and emotional limitations of their love. Compassionate love happens in the midst of acknowledged disability. Kelly knows her days are numbered in community. There is resignation in her story, her movements, and her unfortunate spill on the front steps. The potential for discouragement is elevated in these moments. Doug is deeply fatigued following months of community upheaval and recent disappointment. His reflections are theologically rich, invoking the Christian notion of atonement, or God's healing of humanity through resurrection. Yet his reflection is hardly triumphal. Doug's reference to God is raw and seasoned with fatalism. He is running on fumes. The discipline of compassionate love is granular and prickly. Practitioners must face their limitations on the ground and in the pew. By marking the human bounds of creativity, contentment, and meaning, disability is a difficult and sometimes unwelcome tutor. Compassionate love is humanly resigned to the uncertainty of fragile earthen vessels.

Third, durable compassionate love requires practitioners to find *meaning* in action. Questions regarding this aspect are sprinkled throughout the vignettes. Where is God in community? What are the consequences of my physical suffering? Why mental illness? The everyday problems of L'Arche vacillate between challenging and overwhelming.

Without meaning, the fragile ark is easily pushed sideways in the deepening trough. Seeking a meaningful place in community, Avram expends great effort to fit into the card game. Working through the implications of his recent visit to L'Arche in Ireland, Adam tries to reframe the meaning of downward mobility and everyday simplicity. Confronted with the volatility of bipolar disorder, Alan reaches into his nautical experience to find a sustaining metaphor. From candle ritual to Guadalupe road, L'Arche intentionally considers the meaning of compassionate love and its origins in disability. This meaning is both religious and scientific. It is abstract, concrete, and even trivial. It is Katherine's transforming moment, Dominique's concern for Tessa, and pepperoni pizza saved for Doug.

Compassionate love in L'Arche makes more with less. Community members are masters of adaptation and flexibility. Financial and personnel concerns identified through my conversation with Sophia are counterbalanced with commitment of core members and assistants to the movement. L'Arche may be impossible, but this does not diminish its ongoing possibility. Each community recognizes the rare beauty of compassionate potential and its miraculous realization in the midst of disability. L'Arche members who ascribe to the discipline of compassionate love are willing to grapple with financial and personnel concerns. The water is cold. Immediate solutions may for a time remain elusive. It is dark in the trough between waves. Eventually, however, L'Arche rises to the crest. The view is breathtaking. Landmarks are visible toward safe harbor. Compassionate love lives on the cusp of redemption identified through Doug's narrative, God's wild card that is already and not yet.[3]

White elephant

The research project is finished. I am sitting with two core members and six caregiver assistants in the last community on my travel itinerary. We are in the spacious living room of an old Victorian mansion. The conversation is lively and good fun. The jokes are inclusive, the humor piquant. Yet there is a white elephant in the room. One of the long-term assistants is preparing to leave. Tina is revered in this community, a fixture after years of service. The laughter is bittersweet and colored with pained recognition that L'Arche faces inevitable change. Compassionate love in L'Arche must repeatedly contend with tumult and insecurity. Unexpectedly, the white elephant is named. With a nod toward the pending departure of her colleague, Diane asks the group several questions. Her manner unconsciously adopts the posture of clinical psychologist – empathy directed toward clients grappling with anticipatory grief:

> What is the greatest lesson from your time in L'Arche? What have community challenges taught you? Are you changed because of your experiences?

*　　*　　*

Trevor is sitting directly across from Diane. He unconsciously shifts on the couch, thinking hard. Abruptly he sits up straight, speaking rapidly and with conviction.

> I would say that experience with conflict has influenced my ability to live in L'Arche, to stay in L'Arche; not necessarily the conflict itself, but my ability to stick with it. It is difficult to live with other people and not to give up on it. A common reaction of mine when living with difficult situations used to be avoidance. 'Well, I know all of the things that I want to change, but I will do it the next time.' I'd put things off. Try to avoid the conflict. Experience has given me both the strength and the desire to try and change things when I am in the midst of the situation. It is hard to try and change things, but I think it is much more difficult if you keep putting it off. It's funny, but the experience of conflict gave me the courage to face more conflict, not run away. I still have a lot to learn, but I think in terms of my awareness and needed growth, it helped.

Tina is attentive to Trevor, nodding and smiling in agreement. When he finishes, she pulls herself up. The group moves closer to listen. Core member Gracie curls an arm around Tina's shoulders. The assistant suddenly reaches for a tissue.

> It's been quite an amazing year. I'm still trying to come to terms with the fact I'm leaving next month. It's hard to leave. I don't want to lose these people, I love them so much and have learned so much about myself and learned about what it means to truly love somebody and be loved and be in relationship with people. The intentionality of living a daily life. I'm going to miss reflecting after dinner with the core members and assistants. I'm going to miss the simple joy of being with the core members and going out into the community with them. I can

still do that – I hope that I continue to do it. This is what I need right now, to really work on taking care of myself. [long silence, weeping] It's hard to do that when you're an assistant. I know that this feels like the right decision for me, I hear the voice saying, 'Go on. It'll always be here. You can come back. It's OK to go and be present with yourself for a while. L'Arche has taught you that.' With other jobs or professions I'd be thinking, 'They'll never want me back if I quit.' But it's not quitting here, it's listening and discerning. Things are totally different.

The conversation pauses for more than a minute. Neighbors place supportive hands on Tina's shoulder and knee. The Regulator clock on the wall ticks toward noon. Diane breaks the silence with uncharacteristic solemnity. Her words are slow.

I came to a point where I realized we are really connected. Love connects us. It is a connection between faith and how you live your whole life. Not to compartmentalize your faith and spirituality apart from your career. Instead, I've learned to incorporate those deepest beliefs and values intimately through community life. It is not a job – L'Arche is really a vocation or a ministry. It is also a sense of mutuality. The assistants get more from the core members than they could ever give. I really struggle when people reject L'Arche or, worse, go on about what a special person I must be in order to do this work. 'That is so nice of you!' It's that whole idea that I'm the caregiver and I'm taking care of these poor, disadvantaged people. Where does the misinformation come from? It's simply not true in L'Arche. Community life is such a mutual thing and we are receiving so much from the core members and not just being selfless caregivers.

Erin is watching and listening with rapt attention. Her response pours out quickly, contents slightly under pressure. While she speaks, Gracie quietly begins to hum an old hymn. It might be 'When I Survey the Wondrous Cross'.

You're asking great questions which go right to the heart of what L'Arche means. I'm thinking of several moments, but one really stands out. Some of you might remember. Phil [Erin's husband] came out to visit me in Ohio. We were in the long-distance relationship phase, before we were engaged. It was a horrible visit. We decided to take a

break. Break up, take a break, whatever. We were in Cleveland at the
time, sitting at the beach on the rocks, watching Lake Erie. A storm
had passed through and the waves were big and a little scary. I had a
moment looking at the water with Phil sitting right there and realized
that in so many ways I was quite a child. I hadn't before realized that.
I realized how infantile parts of me were. I wasn't growing very much.
But it was kind of a shocking thing to realize. Because I was getting
older and life might easily pass me by. It wasn't just a theoretical or
philosophical idea. When you are 17 you don't think about such
things. Right, you have barely gone through puberty. But here I was,
getting on in my late 20s, not doing much with life, not really growing.
It was a big moment for me, watching the waves. I remember that
moment vividly. I realized it wasn't just about me being content.
Already I was pretty content. I had faith, I worshipped in church.
I wasn't that different from how I am now; it's just that I wasn't
growing. I still have a lot of house cleaning to do. These days the community keeps me cleaning house, it keeps things growing. What that
epiphany did was help me be less self-centered. It wouldn't have
happened if I wasn't in L'Arche. Funny thing, L'Arche is not something that I think fits terribly well with my gifts, but it is something I
am grateful to be doing. It challenges me to grow, to really live.

Nadia is sitting on the floor cross-legged, like a yoga master. Today she is
dressed entirely in black, familiar turquoise visible on the chain around
her neck. Reserved throughout the conversation, she is suddenly alive.

I'm thinking of the moment when I told my dad I was heading for
L'Arche instead of med school at Tulane. My mom was in the room
too. I tried to help them understand how I felt. I told them that most
of my life was spent trying not to offend them. I have a lot of practice
trying to see what other people want or expect of me. Finally I'm
making a decision for what I think is important. Of course it didn't go
over very well. But it was a huge step forward in my life. It's a big part
of my work in L'Arche. I'm trying to keep that new maturity in play. I
try to be very clear about what I'm feeling about community. To tell
others clearly, 'For me this is not OK, but I'm still interested in how
you feel.' We can have different values and beliefs and can still come
together. Everyone can profit as long as we respect each other's values,
recognizing what is yours and making sure that we talk about it with
love. We don't have to force the other people to think that my per-

spective is the right one. This is the key to L'Arche because there are
so many different people from different ages and different countries,
different backgrounds, and different religious beliefs. It can be really
enriching and really positive.

Until this moment, Randall sits quietly on the sofa. His massive form
dominates one corner of the room. As he opens his mouth to speak, the
house becomes utterly silent. Randall is the soul of the community, a
mountain of steady conviction and trustworthiness.

Leaving is tough. For me, the greatest lesson came through the process
of leaving the Jesuits. Not knowing whether I should leave or not. At
the same time it was a very strengthening thing. No sooner had
Patricia and I made the decision and gone public than somebody told
us that it was the work of Satan. We couldn't believe it. What a
terrible thing to say. In a way it was more confirmation for me that
this was the right decision. It put things in perspective for me. I'm
really struggling with Tina's leaving. L'Arche is going through a period
of maintaining what is essential. One of the things that L'Arche has
taught me is that we all have a brokenness that can never be fixed, no
matter what other people might do. Doctors, psychologists, and even
clergy can't fix us. In L'Arche there is a profound consensus regarding
the void and that only God can fill the void. Part of our role is to help
others come to realize that. In the process, you learn about your own
dark spots, some holes that can never be repaired. I feel that sometimes, especially in America, the way of looking at reality is that we're
the best and brightest and we can find within ourselves the resources
to do anything we want to do. The notion of humbly walking with
God is pushed off on religious freaks and people on the margins. That
kind of stuff doesn't apply any more. Somehow discovering our own
self-esteem will ultimately solve the problem. So we should look for
every opportunity with each core member to develop their self-esteem.
At one level that's fine. But it only goes so far, and then there's a
point where there needs to be some reflection on our brokenness. It's
a difficult thing in L'Arche. We share this intense experience and then
we leave. The experience and people who shared it will never be forgotten.

*   *   *

The inner voice

The van hurtles over the interstate. Hospitable to the last, the community sends me to the airport with two of its most precious members. Randall is driving, skillfully weaving through building rush-hour traffic. Gracie rides shotgun, scrutinizing a map of the area. Navigation is not her principal objective. Rather, she makes a fine game connecting landmarks, intersections, and neighborhoods with notations on the map. In several instances we discover things and places which are not recorded by the map company. We must make a better map. Gracie asks me if I will pencil in the appropriate cartographic revisions. Doing my best against the bumps in the road, I draw small icons at Gracie's behest. A few miles of this partnership yields dividends. The map now includes a local sugar factory, the metropolitan police station, and a distinctive water tower. We have found the SPCA and an urban hospital. The map is revised for the benefit of present and future voyagers. Gracie brandishes her scroll with the confidence of Shackleton nearing Antarctica. We know where we are going.

Randall takes the airport exit, deftly avoiding road construction and merging tractor trailers. A steady procession of airliners makes final approach to the main runway. These are obscured as we pull up to the terminal. People and baggage are everywhere. We get out of the van, taking care to make sure Gracie is well away from danger on the sidewalk. Randall removes my luggage from the cargo area, placing bags in a row by the curb. As we say our goodbyes, he places a small book in my hand. The book is covered with rough-hewn material which feels like aspen bark. A compass rose is stenciled onto the surface. Inside are blank pages of homemade paper. Flax seeds, plant stems, and other organic materials are visible in the fibrous lavender parchment. The book is a diary, likely crafted in the L'Arche workshop affiliated with this community. I am startled by an enormous hand which grips my right shoulder. Randall's kind blue eyes are unwavering in his presentation of this gift, a benediction which upholds the great secret of L'Arche.

L'Arche is a place of instinctively knowing the inner voice of God. It's a voice that is quietly present through the ups and downs. You know when you are not supposed to do something, or that you should do something. You must trust the voice even though it logically makes no sense. Even if your stomach is upset or your blood pressure is rising and it makes no sense; to still trust the inner voice. It's an openness and opportunity for trust. Your trust will be illogical like L'Arche and absolutely crazy like L'Arche, but you know how much it matters. Something so deeply inside that you want to jerk against it. I wanted to jerk my knee in response to what I was hearing in my old life. They offered me treasures in my first job, anything to keep me there. At the time I was saying to myself, 'Why would I walk away from this? Why would I leave a great career and live in L'Arche?' But I kept listening to the inner voice. Everyone around me was screaming, 'Why are you doing this, what are you doing?' It was that inner voice of God, telling me to walk away without really knowing what comes next. It was the voice of grace. It was the voice which calls me beloved and compels me to love others.

Acknowledgements

I am grateful for the friendship and assistance of many individuals associated with the project. Heartfelt thanks are extended to the core members, assistants, and leadership of L'Arche USA. While anonymous in this book, I remember each of these wonderful people by name. The American L'Arche zone took a measured risk in welcoming a young researcher. I am indebted for the opportunity. I especially thank Jean Vanier, who discerned the value of a book-length work on compassionate love and disability in L'Arche.

Thanks to Warren S. Brown at the Graduate School of Psychology, Fuller Theological Seminary: friend, mentor, and fly-fishing partner. Warren pointed to the Fetzer grant opportunity and supplied practical wisdom along the way. My deepest gratitude remains with Lawrence J. Walker at the University of British Columbia: friend and postdoctoral mentor in moral psychology. His fingerprints cover every aspect of project design. I have never met another researcher of Larry's expertise, nor of his character. The book belongs to him.

I greatly appreciate Heidi Ihrig, Wayne Ramsey, and Lynn Underwood at the Fetzer Institute who generously funded the project. Thanks to Mary Ann Meyers and Charles Harper of the John Templeton Foundation who funded a breakthrough symposium on L'Arche and disability at Trosly-Breuil, France, in 2007. The symposium involved wonderful dialogue partners in Pamela Cushing, Bill Gaventa, Hans Reinders, and John Swinton. Thanks also to Norman Giesbrecht who shared passion for L'Arche and compassionate love.

The book project received early endorsement from Stephen G. Post at the State University of New York at Stony Brook and Robert A. Emmons at the University of California, Davis; outstanding scholars and leaders in the positive psychology movement. Stephen's persistent and smiling encouragement kept me focused. Bob's scholarly example reminded me of hopeful possibilities. My deep admiration is with these fine individuals and their work on love and gratitude.

I am grateful for the first Beverly Hardcastle Stanford Fellowship at Azusa Pacific University which provided release time for compilation of research materials and writing. The sabbatical permitted efficient development of the manuscript. The award included an unexpected bonus – partnership with excellent colleagues and administrators including Mark Eaton, Carole Lambert, Rosemary Liegler, Mark Stanton, and Robert K. Welsh. Finally, I thank Beverly Hardcastle Stanford for her unwavering support of qualitative methods in applied behavioral research.

My sincere gratitude is extended to Caroline Chartres at Continuum Publishing Group in London, who enthusiastically adopted the book concept and steered it to publication. Caroline is experienced, gracious, and competent; paramount traits for editorial excellence. Thanks to research assistants Lauren V. Adelchanow, Susan M. Kroeker, and Nancy Williams who worked tirelessly on transcription and coding. The L'Arche project generated some 1,400 pages of interview data. The efforts of these dedicated individuals prevented a scholarly drowning.

I thank the collective wisdom of others for insight into love and altruism. Special thanks to my fellow STARS grant recipients Warren S. Brown, Gregory Peterson, Michael L. Spezio, and James Van Slyke, partners in the scientific study of virtue. Thanks to STARS consultants Ralph Adolphs and Colin Camerer at the California Institute of Technology, and Linda Trinkaus Zagzebski at the University of Oklahoma. Finally, thanks to Phillip R. Shaver at the University of California, Davis, who kindly indicated the importance of attachment in L'Arche.

Thanks to the Rev. David Abdo, David and Tamara Atkins, Bryan Cosby, the Rev. Greg Ehlert, the Rev. Jamie Evans, the Rev. Rick Lemberg, M. Kyle Matsuba, Ryan McKenzie, the Rev. Lana Roberts, Rob Simpson, Dustin Smucker, and David Williams, who provided encouragement and intellectual sustenance. Thanks to Doug and Joanie Stude, who never ceased to believe in the project. I am grateful to my doctoral students at Azusa Pacific University who wrestled with the implications of compassionate love, altruism, and the brain. Finally, thanks to Craig A. Boyd, who kept the agapic prerogatives of L'Arche squarely in view.

I am grateful for the support of gifted office administrators. Karen Akers, Jacki Deyo, and Sheri Myers in the Department of Graduate Psychology who kept things upright against wind and waves. Thanks to colleagues David Brokaw, Joy Bustrum, Charles Chege, Stephen Cheung, Holli Eaton, Marv Erisman, Vicki Ewing, Marjorie Graham-Howard, Beth Houskamp, Sheryn Scott, Bobbi Thomas, Theresa Tisdale, and

Diane Puchbauer for their support. The greatest academic opportunities are discovered collectively.

Thanks to Al Dueck and Katharine Meese Putman at the Graduate School of Psychology, Fuller Theological Seminary. These friends invited presentations on L'Arche as part of the 2003 and 2006 integration symposia. Resulting interactions with other presenters, faculty, and students proved invaluable. Thanks to Delores Friesen, James Holm, James Pankratz, and David Rose for sharing the journey. My first stumbling steps in academia were steadied by these individuals and their conviction that L'Arche was a worthy pursuit.

My deepest thanks are for family; David and Fern Ameel, JoEllen Barton, Tony Burke, Kelly Reimer, Richard and Heather Reimer, and Tracy Snell. I am grateful to my daughters, Naomi and Danielle, who never complained when Dad was traveling or staring at the computer. Finally, I am indebted to my wife Lynn, who cheerfully read every word of the manuscript with helpful suggestions for improvement. Lynn made great sacrifices to facilitate hours of research and travel. Without her, the project would not have happened.

Notes

Chapter 1

1   Christina Rossetti, 'The Convent Threshold', in Elizabeth Jennings (ed.), *A Choice of Christina Rossetti's Verse* (London: Faber & Faber, 1970), p. 53.

2   Down's syndrome results from an extra chromosome. The disability is associated with recognizable physical features and variations in mental ability.

3   L'Arche is located in more than 30 countries worldwide. The movement began in the early 1960s, founded by Jean Vanier and Fr Thomas Philippe in Trosly-Breuil, France.

4   See Eric R. Pianka, *Evolutionary Ecology*, 6th edition (New York: Cummings, 1999).

5   See C. Daniel Batson, 'Addressing the altruism question experimentally', in Stephen Post, Lynn Underwood, Jeffrey Schloss, and William Hurlbut (eds), *Altruism and Altruistic Love: Science, Philosophy, and Religion in Dialogue* (New York: Oxford University Press, 2002), pp. 89–105. Batson argues that altruism and compassionate love are grounded in empathy. Without question empathy is important to compassionate love. Yet equanimity between empathy and compassionate love may oversimplify what is happening in L'Arche. Chapter 5 will expand this discussion further.

6   Behavioral economist Colin Camerer notes a subgroup of individuals who consistently give real money to the public good despite evidence that others are profiting. The greed of others does not deter charitable 'saints'. To his surprise, these individuals fully understand their actions and consequences. Yet they continue to give. This group comprises 3 to 5 per cent of the general population. I am currently involved in research exploring reasons for their behavior.

7   See Steven J. Sandage, Kaye V. Cook, Peter C. Hill, Brad D. Strawn, and Kevin S. Reimer, 'Hermeneutics and psychology: A review and dialectical model', *Review of General Psychology* 12 (2008), pp. 344–64. This article details hermeneutical realism in behavioral science. Also, Eranda Jayawickreme and Anthony Chemero, 'Ecological moral realism: An alternative framework for studying moral psychology', *Review of General Psychology* 12 (2008), pp. 118–26.

8   A timely trend in behavioral science is the study of environmental (ecological) factors which influence moral behaviors such as compassionate love. See Jorge Moll, Roland Zahn, Ricardo de Oliveira-Souza, Frank Krueger, and Jordan Grafman, 'The neural basis of human moral cognition', *Nature Reviews Neuroscience* 6 (2005), pp. 799–809.

9   'Non-reductive' refers to a view of behavior as multifaceted, contextually nested, and dynamic. Scientists embracing this perspective are skeptical that behavior is fully understood at the level of neurons or neurotransmitters. For a detailed discussion, see Nancey Murphy and Warren S. Brown, *Did My Neurons Make Me Do It? Philosophical and Neurobiological Perspectives on Moral Responsibility and Free Will* (New York: Oxford University Press, 2007). Also, Raymond W. Gibbs, *Embodiment and Cognitive Science* (New York: Cambridge University Press, 2005).

10   See William Damon and Daniel Hart, *Self-Understanding in Childhood and Adolescence* (New York: Cambridge University Press, 1991). Also, Daniel Hart and Suzanne Fegley, 'Prosocial behavior and caring in adolescence: Relations to self-understanding and social judgment', *Child Development* 66 (1995), pp. 1346–59.

11 Kübler-Ross was a Swiss psychiatrist known for her stage-like model of responses to impending death. See Elisabeth Kübler-Ross, *On Death and Dying* (New York: Scribner's, 1997).

12 See Parker Palmer, *Let Your Life Speak: Listening for the Voice of Vocation* (San Francisco: Jossey-Bass, 1999).

Chapter 2

1 Martin Luther King Jr, *Strength to Love* (New York: Harper, 1963).

2 I do not mean to imply that the candle ritual speaks in the same way to these individuals.

3 See Terrence W. Deacon, *The Symbolic Species: The Co-Evolution of Language and the Brain* (New York: Norton, 1997). Deacon makes a compelling argument for symbolic reference as the adaptive innovation which makes language possible. Symbol lives at the root of religious language and meaning. I believe that symbolic reference is operative for even the most mentally limited core members, at least to the extent that collective associations are made between basic emotions and routine behaviors around artifacts such as the candle.

4 See Edwin Hutchins, *Cognition in the Wild* (Cambridge, MA: MIT/Bradford, 1996). A former MacArthur Fellow, Hutchins' argument for 'distributed cognition' is influential in the fields of neuroscience and philosophy. I have avoided scientific jargon to make Hutchins' argument transparent. Also, Andy Clark, *Being There: Putting Brain, Body, and World Back Together Again* (Cambridge, MA: MIT, 1997).

5 See Lev S. Vygotsky, *Thought and Language: Revised Edition* (Cambridge, MA: MIT, 1986). This work was first published in Russian. An English translation became available in 1962.

6 Hutchins makes no connection between distributed cognition and religion. Responsibility for this discussion is entirely my own. See Kevin S. Reimer, 'Fiat lux: Religion as distributed cognition', *Journal of Psychology and Christianity* 24 (2005), pp. 130–39. A number of ideas and concepts in this chapter have origins in this article.

7 I offer this perspective on religious experience in the candle ritual for descriptive purposes. In psychology, religion is commonly understood on instrumental (i.e. functional) grounds. Examples readily garner media attention, namely that religion makes marriages happier and speeds recovery time from surgery. I find this approach naïve to the symbolic complexity of religious language and meaning. Instrumentalism potentially demeans the authenticity of faith as an individual and collective response to God. See Alvin C. Dueck and Kevin S. Reimer, *A Peaceable Psychology* (Grand Rapids, MI: Brazos, 2009).

8 Larry Walker is professor of psychology at the University of British Columbia, Vancouver, Canada.

9 Crystal Cathedral, Garden Grove, California.

10 Informed consent was obtained for all vignettes and exchanges in this book, including those recorded outside the conventional interview protocol.

Chapter 3

1 This quote is taken from unpublished letters of Jean Vanier to the L'Arche communities of Canada. His full remarks are found at www.larchecanada.org/jeanlet1.htm.

2 An excellent summary of compassionate love is found in Stephen Post, 'The tradition of agapé', in Stephen Post, Lynn Underwood, Jeffrey Schloss, and William Hurlbut (eds), *Altruism and Altruistic Love: Science, Philosophy, and Religion in Dialogue* (New York: Oxford University Press, 2002), pp. 51–63.

3 'Katherine' is a pseudonym. Additional portions of Katherine's story are published in Jack O. Balswick, Pamela King, and Kevin S. Reimer, *The Reciprocating Self* (Downer's Grove, IL: InterVarsity, 2005).

4 An integration of scientific and religious perspectives on altruism can be found in Thomas Oord, *The Altruism Reader: Selections from Writings on Love, Religion, and Science* (Philadelphia: Templeton Foundation Press, 2007).

5 See Don S. Browning, 'Science and religion on the nature of love', in Stephen Post, Lynn Underwood, Jeffrey Schloss, and William Hurlbut (eds), *Altruism and Altruistic Love: Science, Philosophy, and Religion in Dialogue* (New York: Oxford University Press, 2002), pp. 335–45.

Several ideas for this chapter were first published in Kevin S. Reimer, 'Agape, brokenness, and theological realism in L'Arche', in Craig Boyd (ed.), *Visions of Agape* (Aldershot: Ashgate, 2008), pp. 85-101.

6   See Stephen Drigotas, Caryl Rusbult, Jennifer Wieselquist, and Sarah Whitton, 'Close partner as sculptor of the ideal self: Behavioral affirmation and the Michelangelo phenomenon', *Journal of Personality and Social Psychology* 77 (1999), pp. 293-323.

7   The authors note that this process is both conscious and unconscious depending upon situation. In elderly couples, many of these behaviors become routine in a manner providing a consistent scaffold of compassionate love.

8   See Jonathan Haidt and Frederik Bjorklund, 'Social intuitionists answer six questions about moral psychology', in W. Sinnott-Armstrong (ed.), *Moral Psychology, Volume 3* (Cambridge, MA: MIT Bradford, 2008), pp. 181-217. Also, Jonathan Haidt, 'The new synthesis in moral psychology', *Science* 316 (2007), pp. 998-1002. The matter of intuition and moral behavior will be considered at greater length in Chapter 5.

9   Dietrich Bonhoeffer was a German pastor and theologian who opposed Nazism. He is perhaps best known for his writings on community in *Life Together* (San Francisco: Harper-One, 1978).

10 Motivation is a complex topic in psychology. My purpose in this chapter is to consider the social and communal aspects of compassionate love as virtue.

11 In this sense, presence closely resembles work in social psychology on *attachment*. Attachment theory suggests that early bonds established between parents and children orient our ability to form lasting and trusting relationships. See Mario Mikulincer and Phillip R. Shaver, *Attachment in Adulthood: Structure, Dynamics, and Change* (New York: Guilford, 2007).

Chapter 4

1   See William James, *Varieties of Religious Experience: A Study in Human Nature* (New York: BiblioBazaar, 1902/2007), p. 231.

2   See John Calvin, *Institutes of the Christian Religion, Vol. 2* (Philadelphia: Westminster John Knox, 1559/1960), p. 1132.

3   MRI stands for 'magnetic resonance imaging'. Best known as a medical diagnostic for soft tissues, MRI machines are fueling a renaissance in the science of the brain.

4   See Lawrence Kohlberg, *Essays on Moral Development: Volume 1, The Philosophy of Moral Development* (San Francisco: Harper & Row, 1981). Also, Lawrence Kohlberg, *Essays on Moral Development: Volume 2, The Psychology of Moral Development* (San Francisco: Harper & Row, 1984).

5   See Lawrence J. Walker and Russell Pitts, 'Naturalistic conceptions of moral maturity', *Developmental Psychology* 34 (1998), pp. 403-23. In a reaction to Kohlberg, Walker argues that moral behavior references ordinary conceptions of good conduct which resemble virtues. Not surprisingly, some conceptions may arise in conjunction with religious or spiritual influences. Also, Lawrence J. Walker and Kevin S. Reimer, 'The relationship between moral and spiritual development', in Peter Benson, Pamela King, Linda Wagener, and Eugene Roehlkepartain (eds), *The Handbook of Spiritual Development in Childhood and Adolescence* (Newbury Park, CA: Sage, 2005), pp. 265-301.

6   Jonathan Haidt is the best-known advocate of this argument. See Jonathan Haidt and Frederik Bjorklund, 'Social intuitionists answer six questions about moral psychology', in W. Sinnott-Armstrong (ed.), *Moral Psychology: Volume 3* (Cambridge, MA: MIT, 2008), pp. 181-217.

7   Haidt was joined by Richard Shweder in making this critique. See Jonathan Haidt, Silvia Koller, and Maria Dias, 'Affect, culture, and morality, Or is it wrong to eat your dog?', *Journal of Personality and Social Psychology* 65 (1993), pp. 613-28. Also, Richard Shweder, Nancy Much, Manamohan Mahapatra, and Lawrence Park, 'The "Big Three" of morality (autonomy, community, divinity) and the "Big Three" explanations of suffering', in A. Brandt and P. Rozin (eds), *Morality and Health* (Florence, KY: Taylor & Francis/Routledge, 1997), pp. 119-69. A rejoinder from the rights and justice perspective is found in

Elliot Turiel and Cecilia Wainryb, 'Social reasoning and the varieties of social experiences in cultural contexts', in H. Reese (ed.), *Advances in Child Development and Behavior: Volume 25* (San Diego, CA: Academic Press, 1994), pp. 289–326.

8   See Hanna Damasio, 'Impairment of interpersonal social behavior caused by acquired brain damage', in S. Post, L. Underwood, J. Schloss, and W. Hurlbut (eds), *Altruism and Altruistic Love: Science, Philosophy, and Religion in Practice* (New York: Oxford University Press, 2002), pp. 264–71.

9   See Anne Colby and William Damon, *Some Do Care: Contemporary Lives of Moral Commitment* (New York: Free Press, 1992).

10   See Daniel Hart, Robert Atkins, and Debra Ford, 'Urban America as a context for the development of moral identity in adolescence', *Journal of Social Issues 54* (1998), pp. 513–30.

11   See Joshua Greene, R. Brian Sommerville, Leigh Nystrom, John Darley, and Jonathan Cohen, 'An MRI investigation of emotional engagement in moral judgment', *Science 293* (2001), pp. 2105–8.

12   See Owen Flanagan, *Varieties of Moral Personality: Ethics and Psychological Realism* (Cambridge, MA: Harvard, 1991).

13   See Kevin S. Reimer, 'Natural character: Psychological realism for the downwardly mobile', *Theology & Science 2* (2004), pp. 89–105.

14   See Dan P. McAdams, *The Stories We Live By: Personal Myths and the Making of the Self* (New York: Guilford, 1997).

15   See Henri J. M. Nouwen, *The Wounded Healer: Ministry in Contemporary Society* (New York: Image, 1979).

16   See Omri Gillath, Phillip Shaver, Mario Mikulincer, Rachel Nitzberg, Ayelet Erez, and Marinus Van Ijzendoorn, 'Attachment, caregiving, and volunteering: Placing volunteerism in an attachment theoretical framework', *Personal Relationships 12* (2005), pp. 425–46.

Chapter 5

1   See Job 2:8 (New Revised Standard Version).

2   Up to this point, the book emphasizes participant-observer ethnography and interviews. This chapter introduces case study as a method of inquiry. Several ideas and concepts for this chapter were first published in Kevin S. Reimer, 'Moral transformation in L'Arche communities for the developmentally disabled', in Hans Reinders (ed.) *Learning from the Disabled* (Grand Rapids, MI: Eerdmans, 2009).

3   Although we might illustrate growth from shame toward moral maturity through other assistant narratives, Tina's story offers a clear and articulate example. My decision to focus on a single narrative is aimed at providing a more detailed level of discussion complementary to the survey approach taken throughout the book.

4   See Lawrence Kohlberg, *Essays on Moral Development: Volume 2, The Psychology of Moral Development* (San Francisco: Harper & Row, 1984). Also, Elliot Turiel, *The Development of Social Knowledge: Morality and Convention* (New York: Cambridge University Press, 1983). Turiel argues that morality is confined to domains of knowledge in *harm*, *rights*, and *justice*. Finally, Steven R. Quartz and Terrence J. Sejnowski, *Liars, Lovers, and Heroes: What the New Brain Science Reveals About How We Become Who We Are* (New York: Harper, 2003). Quartz and Sejnowski believe that morality is principally about the anticipated consequences of our actions, a position known as *consequentialism*.

5   See Anne Colby and William Damon, *Some Do Care: Contemporary Lives of Moral Commitment* (New York: Free Press, 1992).

6   Typical examples of social desirability bias include desire to conceal racial prejudice, underreport risky sexual behavior, or exaggerate personal generosity through charitable giving.

7   Aquinas was a medieval Catholic philosopher and theologian. Aquinas relied heavily on the philosophy of Aristotle, famed student of Plato in ancient Greece.

8   A former student of Turiel voiced confusion to me regarding this point after a conference presentation on L'Arche. To be sure, I could morally interpret compassionate love in L'Arche through concepts such as justice or consequences. Yet languages of justice (such as

rights) or consequences are almost non-existent in L'Arche. If compassionate love is even remotely moral, L'Arche challenges science to consider the importance of virtue and character in real-world experience. See Alvin C. Dueck and Kevin S. Reimer, A Peaceable Psychology (Grand Rapids, MI: Brazos, 2009).

9   Our eyes quickly search faces, perceiving subtle changes which tell us about the moral intentions of others. See R. Adolphs, D. Tranel, H. Damasio, and A. Damasio, 'Impaired recognition of emotion in facial expressions following bilateral damage to the human amygdala', Nature 372 (1994), pp. 669-72.

10   Moral maturity is analogous to practical wisdom, or the ability to live well through imitation of others. My colleague Linda Zagzebski refers to this process in terms of phronesis, sometimes translated as 'prudence'. See Linda Trinkaus Zagzebski, Virtues of the Mind: An Inquiry into the Nature of Virtue and the Ethical Foundations of Knowledge (Cambridge: Cambridge University Press, 1998). Also, Alasdair MacIntyre, After Virtue (Notre Dame, IN: University of Notre Dame Press, 1984).

11   These core members are probably able to comprehend such concepts on concrete grounds. However, they are nowhere near the abstractly 'refined' level of understanding by which these concepts are conventionally used to index moral maturity.

12   Again, these individuals are likely able to understand that actions have consequences. But owing to mental disability, they are much limited in the ability to apply this knowledge toward a sophisticated moral framework anticipating future contingencies.

13   See Jonathan Haidt, 'The new synthesis in moral psychology', Science 316 (2007), pp. 998-1002.

14   Haidt is an evolutionary psychologist at the University of Virginia.

15   Other concerns are simmering over the moral intuition argument. Haidt's proposal embraces a problematic dualism between conscious and unconscious processes.

16   See June Tangney, 'The moral emotions: Shame, guilt, embarrassment and pride', in T. Dalgleish and M. Power (eds), Handbook of Cognition and Emotion (New York: John Wiley, 1999), pp. 541-68. I am using the terms 'feeling' and 'emotion' interchangeably for simplicity of argument. Some have noted that these are not always identical. 'Feeling' refers to our experience of underlying neurological and physiological changes in body states known as 'emotion'. See Antonio Damasio, Descartes' Error (New York: Vintage, 1994/2006).

17   See Michael Mascolo and Kurt Fischer, 'Developmental transformations in appraisals for pride, shame, and guilt', in June Tangney and Kurt Fischer (eds), Moral Emotions: The Psychology of Shame, Guilt, Embarrassment, and Pride (New York: Guilford, 1995), pp. 64-113.

18   Keen readers will note that shame and guilt reflect elements of disgust. Certainly Tina's feelings identified as 'ugly', 'awful', and 'icky' sound like expressions of disgust. Her description of shame, however, is considerably more complex and nuanced. This is no accident. Brain studies have shown that disgust arises in a part of the brain known as the anterior insula (AI). A highly specific AI region is activated in response to disgusting smells or disgust in the face of another. However, when we are confronted by complex social situations, AI organizes emotion complexes reflecting experience of shame, guilt, and pride. Thus the role of the AI shifts depending on the nature of information processing. Only in the second scenario do empathy and compassionate love become real possibilities. Disgust offers an important, if incomplete account of feelings associated with moral maturity. See B. Wicker, C. Keysers, J. Plailly, J. Royet, V. Gallese, and G. Rizzolatti, 'Both of us disgusted in my insula: The common neural basis of seeing and feeling disgust', Neuron 40 (2003), pp. 655-64. Also, Christian Keysers, 'Insula's function and connectivity during empathic observation, imagination, and experience of emotions', paper presented at the annual meeting of Cognitive Neuroscience Society, April 12-15, 2008, San Francisco, California.

19   See Anne Colby and William Damon, Some Do Care: Contemporary Lives of Moral Commitment (New York: Free Press, 1992).

20   See Antonio Damasio, Descartes' Error (New York: Vintage, 1994/2006).

21   People with a coherent moral self tend to demonstrate consistent priorities linking past, present, and future. See Kevin S. Reimer and David Wade-Stein, 'Moral identity in adoles-